THE

INDIAN SAINT

THE

INDIAN SAINT;

OR,

BUDDHA AND BUDDHISM:

A SKETCH,

HISTORICAL AND CRITICAl.

BY

CHARLES D. B. MILLS.

GYAN

Published by

Gyan Publishing House
5, Ansari Road
Daryaganj, New Delhi-110002
Phone: 011-47034999, 9811692060
E-mail: books@gyanbooks.com

Distribution Network
gyanbooks.com
India, USA, Canada, UK, Australia

ISBN: 978-81-212-5993-4 (PB)
First Published, 1876

2nd Impression 2024

Printed at: Gyan Press, Delhi.

THE INDIAN SAINT
Author: CHARLES D. B. MILLS

THE

INDIAN SAINT;

OR,

BUDDHA AND BUDDHISM:

A SKETCH,

HISTORICAL AND CRITICAL,

BY

CHARLES D. B. MILLS.

NORTHAMPTON, MASS.
JOURNAL AND FREE PRESS CO.
1876.

PREFACE.

The following pages have been written in a feeling ot cordial interest, indeed of love and admiration for the historical character they seek in some degree to present and an earnest desire to render both to him and the faith that has flowed from his thought and life—while abstaining utterly, if possible, from any bias or partiality—equal and exact justice. How far, if at all, this desire may have become realization, it must be for the intelligent reader to decide.

It is difficult, very difficult, to penetrate the spirit and genius of a faith so remote, and in many respects foreign to our own, to interpret it, take its measure justly, weigh it well. Still more difficult, perhaps, to one who should have outgrown, in some degree at least, as is hoped, the Christian limitation, to preserve still the perfect poise, to escape prepossession on the other side, and draw the picture without a shade of flattery.

The writing of these pages was done for the most part nearly four years since. Various circumstances, not necessary here to name, have conspired to prevent an earlier publication. Within this intervening time, important contributions upon the Eastern religions have been made, both in this country and Europe, and the horizon of view has constantly been widening. In particular, the work of Mr. Samuel Johnson, (*Oriental Religions*, Boston, 1872), deserves very cordial and honorable mention. Impressed with so broad and catholic a spirit, so kindly, so generous even, in its hospitality to Eastern thought, so careful in research and affluent in learning, so superior in insight and discrimination, so richly and deeply suggestive, it certainly marks, if it does not make, an epoch in these studies. It would seem to leave little to be desired further upon the themes it treats.

But the field is large, and there is room yet for many reapers and gleaners. Long time it must be ere the sheaves shall all have been gathered; long time indeed ere the last word shall have been spoken, and the final judgment made up, upon this or any other of the great historic faiths.

The present moment is opportune. The night is far spent, and the day is at hand. We are outgrowing the Jewish narrowness that has from the beginning been upon all Christendom—the worship of exclusive claims, of dispensation and of person. We are to study all religions in the light of the universal, to measure all, our own included, against the standard of the absolute. Of the enlargements that shall thereby come, the farthest seeing at present, can form no fitting conception. The old hymn will take on new breadth of meaning, and the lines be sung—

> "Let party names no more
> The *human* world o'erspread;"

the new Jerusalem shall descend from God out of Heaven, and the church of Humanity be inaugurated. All the fragments shall be gathered up, there shall be genuine recognition of the divine in history, respect and appreciation everywhere, but idolatry nowhere. The soul, leaving every weight behind, shall urge ever on and on toward the infinite goal.

In the hope that it may in some slight degree aid to open the way for that bright consummation, this little volume is sent forth. It is doubtless very partial and incomplete, marked and perhaps marred with many deficiencies. If it shall serve in any measure to illustrate the subject it seeks to present, if it shall avail at all to incite and quicken, to enlarge the horizon and exalt the tone of life, its ambitions will have been fulfilled.

SYRACUSE, N. Y., Dec. 15th, 1875.

CONTENTS.

SÂKYA-MUNI.

I.

THE LIFE.

IN the Eastern world to-day there bow untold millions of devout worshipers before Buddha; * his statues are in the temples, his adoration is celebrated with incense of sandal-wood and odors of flowers, his birth-place and theatre of action is the holy land of the church of believers, and immense topes in India have been erected over his real or supposed relics. The vast *vihâras* or monasteries, built in the olden-time, have been thronged with monks eager to learn the law, and the successors of them still stand in Ceylon, Birmah, Thibet, Mongolia, China and Japan. No other name is held in such reverence; Buddha is the incarnation, the great messenger from the heavens to men, his word is the supreme gospel, the

* Koeppen, *Religion des Buddha*, I., p. 121, estimates the number at about one-third the entire population of the globe. The same, or about the same, — Fausböll, Bigandet, Berghaus and Prof. Neumann.

way of salvation for all. No other faith has had such a following, none ever spread so quickly so far, or kept for itself stronger hold upon the popular mind.

For about twenty-four centuries now this religion has been current; albeit expelled from the land of its birth it has wide prevalence in Central and Eastern Asia, and gives thus far no sign, to outward seeming, of any dissolution or decay. By the Pacific wave it is borne to our own coast, and we are brought thus face to face with it — perhaps under one of its coarser and more degenerate types, — as one of the practical problems of our time.

It is a phenomenon certainly well worth our study. We have before us, beyond question, the effect of a powerful personality in history; a wave upon the ocean of mind, far extending, and yet unspent. Mr. Beal, who personally has studied it upon Chinese soil, describes it, viewing it, too, from the stand-point of orthodox Christianity, as "one of the most wonderful movements of the human mind in the direction of Spiritual Truth." We ought to be in condition to look at this fact fairly, to read it truly, with a fine appreciation, as well as just critical rigor.

Who was this Buddha, what is the measure of his claim, what his place comparatively among the great saints and benefactors of the world? What was the magnetic charm of that presence and word that seems to have ravished so many souls, and to have left such deep and lasting impress upon the Eastern peoples? What was the quality of his thought and style of his life, and how shall he stand, permanently, in history? These questions are to have some day full answer.

Myth and legend cover also this history, cover it, indeed, as almost no other that we know. The Eastern mind speaks characteristically in hyperbole and figure, and in this case—so has the imagination been wrought upon and intoxicated—it has overlaid the reality with the sports and extravagances of fancy, almost too deep for possible recovery. It is often exceedingly difficult, and sometimes utterly impracticable to separate the fact from the myth, or, rather, to know how much and what is the fact, behind the myth. There are things which nice, careful critics would promptly dismiss as purely mythic, and which, nevertheless, it is not hard to see, have true historic ground and a fine significance.

Gautama Buddha, called afterward also Sâkya-Muni—the monk or hermit of the Sâkyas—was born in the northern part of India, a little north of what is now the province of Oude, probably in the earlier half of the sixth century before Christ. There is very wide difference in the dates given from different sources here. The Thibetans themselves have as many as fourteen, ranging in the extreme limits nearly 2,000 years apart. But the Chinese and Thibetans generally fix the death at not far from 1,000 B. C.; the Chronicle of Cashmere considerably earlier; the Singhalese, with much unanimity, at 543 B. C. But Max Müller* affirms there are good grounds for setting it at 477 B. C., and as Buddha is commonly reputed to have lived seventy-nine years, this would fix his birth at about 556 B. C. There is, however, notoriously great dimness and uncertainty — which is essentially increased in this instance by special causes — overhanging Indian chronology in the early times, and probably we are able to attain here, at best, but an approximation.† The name of the town was Kapilavastu,‡ capital of a small kingdom of the same name, and his father, Suddhodana — "living upon clean food" — was the king, described as a man of distinguished bravery and integrity. He belonged by this descent to the Sâkyas, and these came of the great

---

* *Chips*, I., p. 206. See also Bigandet, p. 319, note.

† See Koeppen, I., pp. 118, 119.

‡ Kapilavastu was in the eastern part of the province of Kosala, and a little north of the Gorackpur of the present day. It was on a stream, Rohini, which near Gorackpur empties into the Rapti.

Solar race, a race very famous in the early annals of India.* His mother, Mâyâdêvî, was distinguished above all women of her time, for her physical beauty, a beauty so ravishing to the eye that she bore familiarly the name Mâyâ, "illusion;" distinguished, withal, still more for her high qualities of soul. She died seven days after the birth of her son, and he was confided for rearing to the care of a maternal aunt.† There was also a miraculous conception in this relation. According to some of the accounts his mother was a virgin, and he was begotten without human intervention; as a beam of light he entered the womb of Mâyâdêvî. His conception, his growth

* Beal, however, advances the opinion that he was of Scythian descent. A branch or clan of this race, he thinks, may have penetrated Northern India, as another did Assyria about this time, and Buddha was born of this blood, a descendant of the Chakravarttins or Wheel Kings, *i. e.*, universal monarchs. Sâkya's directions as to the funeral obsequies to be observed after his death, the cremation of the body, and the subsequent erection of mounds, or topes, in such numbers over India,—all, he deems, indicate a foreign parentage for this saint. See his *Catena*, pp. 128, 129. But this of the directions is very probably a subsequent invention; it certainly comports little with his known character, and especially with the light esteem, almost the contempt, in which he is represented to have held the body. The weight of the evidence seems altogether in favor of the view that he was of the Aryan race and family of the Sâkyas.

† The incarnation and the birth are both represented in the sculptures found upon the remains of the ancient temple at Sanchi. See Fergusson's *Tree and Serpent Worship*, plates xxxiii. and lxv.

and birth were without taint of human impurity or infirmity.

It is worthy of note, in passing, that this seems to have been a fruitful epoch, productive of superior, genuinely great men. Confucius in China, and Pythagoras in Greece (Magna Græcia), both teachers of broad and universal quality, were cotemporary with Buddha. Xenophanes and, following him, the Eleatic school came about the same time; also Heraclitus. A little earlier was Lao Tsze, a sage more exalted perhaps than Confucius, and cotemporary with him was Thales.

In true Oriental style we are told what attention this advent excited in the world of the gods, and what marvels it wrought in the house and kingdom of Suddhodana. The palace swept itself clean, all the birds of Himavat assembled, testifying their joy in song; the gardens bloomed with flowers and the ponds filled with the lotus; scented waters flowed; meats of all kinds covered the tables, and although partaken freely of, knew no diminution; instruments of music, without touch of hand, played, giving forth the finest melodies; caskets of jewels sprang open, displaying of their own accord their treasures, and finally the palace was irradiated with an unearthly splendor, that eclipsed that of the sun and moon. Gods and goddesses came to pay their adoration before him while he was in the womb of Mâyâdêvî, and Indra and Brahma, chiefs of the gods, descended to receive the new-born child in the garden of Lumbinî, and performed for him those offices usually done to the new-born. The old Brahman Asita, dwelling in Himavat, came down to greet the child, read upon his person the thirty-two primary and the eighty secondary marks of the great man, and predicted to the father that this was to be the Buddha. For himself, he grieved that the old age that was already upon him, would not permit him to hear that fine instruction in the law that was to come.

In due time the child was presented in the temple of the gods. All the images started from their seats and prostrated themselves before him, and sang chants in his praise. He grew up a boy of surpassing beauty and of the most extraordinary parts. Placed in the schools of writing, he soon was superior to his masters, and one of them, Visvamitra, frankly owned he had no more he could teach him. He was pensive, reticent, took little part in the sports of his mates, and used frequently to retire by himself into solitudes, where he seemed lost in meditation. One day, going out with his companions for an excursion to a neighboring village, he quietly withdrew alone into the shadows of a deep forest, where he remained a long while. His continued absence occasioned great anxiety to his friends, and a careful search was instituted, in which the king, his father, took part. They found him sitting under the shade of a bamboo tree, rapt and lost in his thoughts.

The tendency in him to withdrawal and solitary reverie gave pain to the courtiers and all his kindred; it was feared the royal family would some day be without issue, and the throne without an occupant. So it was determined that the young man should marry, and it was hoped that in the attractions of family he might be beguiled from his apparent purpose. He demanded seven days for reflection, and at last feeling sure of himself, sure that marriage could not take from him the calmness of thought, nor leisure for meditation, he consented. He imposed certain imperative conditions. The woman for him must not be a frivolous creature, without sobriety or possession. It little signified for the rest what should be her caste. She might belong to the Vaisyas or the Sûdras, equally well as to the Brahmans or Kshatriyas, only she must be endowed with womanly qualities, such as were to be desired in a companion. Such an one at length was found; it was in the person of the beautiful Gopâ, of the family of Sâkyas, daughter of Dandapâni.

But to this union the father objected. He could

not surrender his daughter to a young man, prince though he were, who had the repute of being rather a dreamer, and deficient in manly qualities. A contest was instituted; among five hundred of the young Sâkyas assembled. Gopâ was promised to the one who should excel all the others in certain athletic performance. Gautama easily lead them all in everything; he was the best swimmer, runner, leaper, archer, albeit he had never before practised any of these arts. The archery was certainly good, for we are told that he split with his arrow a hair at the distance of ten miles, though at the time it was dark as night.* Hardly could any one of the young Sâkyas hope to do better.

He did more. He went into feats of mind, showed himself more proficient than the judges even, in writing, arithmetic, logic, knowledge of the Vedas, philosophy, etc. Dandapâni cordially now yielded his consent, and the marriage took place. The union was of the happiest, a true fellowship, a church of saints. Gautama's age, it is said, was sixteen years when he was married to Gopâ.

But there was in this young man a want that no companionship of wife or dearest friend could supply, thoughts that knew only solitude, that visited

---

* Hardy's *Legends and Theories of the Buddhists*, p. 139.

and gave him communion but in retirement from all outward and seen. There were unanswered questions that haunted, present everywhere by night and by day, subtle, vital, that he must take life-long perhaps to ponder. The prince was still pensive, abode much by himself; the gayety of society and the splendors of the court pleased, but they did not fill or captivate him. Evidently he had not been diverted from the early bias he had shown, and which had given such uneasiness to his friends.

"What is our life," he was wont to revolve with himself, "whence is it and whither? It is like an echo, a dream, the note of a lute, the lightning that flashes for an instant, and is gone; none can tell whence it came or whither it goes. All is instability, change, a ceaseless motion,—is naught. But there must be substance somewhere, some reality wherein is duration and rest. If I could know and attain that, I could bring light to man; free myself, I could deliver the world. I could show them the sure gate of immortality. Withdrawn from the thoughts born of the senses and beset with pain and unrest, I would establish them in repose. In making those who are enveloped in deepest ignorance see the clear light of the law, I should give them that fine vision that reads all things, that ray of pure wisdom that has no blemish or decay."

Three incidents, of a kind the most ordinary and unnoticed in the experience of men generally, happening in his experience were most fruitful in results. One day, starting from the eastern gate of the city with a numerous retinue for a ride to the garden of Lumbinî, a place endeared to him by many most sacred associations, he met upon the way an aged man. He was broken, decrepit, covered with wrinkles, his head was white, the veins and muscles stood prominent over his body, his teeth chattered; leaning upon his staff he tottered, scarcely able to walk. "Who is this man?" he asked of the coachman. "He is small and weak, his flesh and his blood are dried up, his muscles stick to his skin, his body is wasted away, he trembles at every step. Is this some peculiar condition of his family, or is it the common lot of all created beings?"

"Sir," replied the coachman, "this man is borne down by old age, all his senses are enfeebled, suffering has destroyed his strength, he is despised by his relations; without support and incapable of anything, he is abandoned, like the dead tree in the forest. But this is no special condition of his family. In every creature youth is overcome by old age. Your father, your mother, all your kindred and friends, shall come to the same state, there is no other end for living beings."

"Alas then," answered the prince, "are creatures so weak, so ignorant and foolish as to be proud of the youth that intoxicates them, not seeing the old age that awaits? For myself, I will away. Coachman, turn my chariot quickly. I, the future prey of old age, what have I to do with pleasure or joy?" And, turning back, he reëntered the city.

Another day, going out as before, he met a sick man, a poor wretch suffering with fever, consumed by the quenchless fire, homeless and friendless, dying in destitution and filth. And again he met a corpse upon a bier, borne by weeping friends, for the tomb. He interrogated his coachman, and learned that these too were under the lot of humanity, and was affected to deepest sadness. He returned to his home, and would go no more in pursuit of pleasure. Once again he met a *bhikshu*, a mendicant. He interrogated his coachman, and was answered, "This man has renounced all pleasures, all desires, and leads a life of severe austerity. *He tries to conquer himself.* He has become a devotee. Without passion and without envy he goes about, seeking alms."

"Well said," replied the prince; "the life of a devotee has always been praised by the wise. It shall be my refuge and the refuge of other creatures; it will lead us to a real life, to happiness and immortality."

His resolution was taken. Gopâ, his wife, was the first to whom he imparted the choice secret. One night she awoke in terror from a bad dream, and asked Gautama for an explanation. He opened to her freely his purpose, sympathized with her grief, and was able for the time to console her in good degree for her loss. Then, filled with filial respect and spirit of submission, he sought the same night the bed-side of his father, told him frankly all and begged to be permitted to depart in peace. The father, with eyes filled with tears, besought him to change his determination. Naught that utmost wish could desire should be withheld from him, the palace, kingdom, servants, the king himself—all should be laid at his feet. But nothing of this could avail with the prince. "Give me," said he, "that I may know the method of exemption from old age, disease, death, or give me at least that I shall know no transmigration in the world beyond, and I will cheerfully remain with thee ever." The king confessed that this was utterly beyond his power; all were subject to that condition; even the Rishis, in the midst of the Kalpa in which they live,* are not exempt from the dread of age.

* The duration of a Kalpa is indicated in this way: "Take a rock forming a cube of about fourteen miles, touch it once in a hundred years with a piece of fine cloth, and the rock will sooner be reduced

The king saw that it was of no avail whatever to attempt to dissuade this youth from his purpose, but he resolved, if possible, to keep him at home, to prevent his escape.* The gates of the city were watched, guards were set all about the town, and Suddhodana himself, with five hundred young Sâkyas, watched at the gate of the palace. But it was all in vain. One night when the guards, weary, were fast asleep, the prince ordered his coachman Tchandaka to saddle his horse, for his hour was come. The faithful coachman, in tears, made one last appeal, begging him not to sacrifice himself thus, his youth and beauty and fine position for the poor life of a devotee. It was an empty word for those ears. "Shunned by the wise, like the fangs of a serpent, cast out like an unclean vessel, the desires, Tchandaka, as I but too well know, are the ruin of all virtue. Let a torrent of thunderbolts, of arrows, flaming swords, like the vivid lightnings, or the burning summit of the volcano, sooner fall upon and overwhelm me, than that I be born again with the desire of house." *

---

to dust than a kalpa will have attained its end."—M. Müller, *Lecture on Buddhist Nihilism*, p. 8.

* Another account has it that at this point Mâra, the tempter, appeared and promised him the kingdom of the world, if he would renounce his design and remain. "But the offer was as repugnant

Unobserved by any, he left the city at the hour of midnight,* and the star Pushya, that had presided at his birth, rose at this moment above the horizon. He turned to cast a last look upon the palace and the town, and touched with a deep tenderness he said, sweetly, "Never shall I return again to this city of Kapila, until I shall have attained the cessation of birth and death, exemption from old age and decay, and reached the pure intelligence." He was not to visit this home again until twelve years afterward, when he came there to preach the new faith. Together they travelled all the night, and at day-break were twelve leagues away. Gautama alighted, dismissed his coachman homeward with his horse, and the costly ornaments that he took from

---

to those ears as would have been the attempt to pierce them with glowing iron."—Koeppen, I., p. 82.

* Some of the legends have it that the departure took place on the night after the birth of his child. Standing upon the threshold of the door, he saw the princess sleeping, with her hand placed over the head of the infant. He wished to remove the hand, that he might look into the little face, but fearing that he might thereby awaken the mother, and his resolution in consequence be weakened, if not destroyed, he refrained. Gazing for a moment from the threshold, with what thoughts we can well imagine, he turned away and left family and court forever. "After having become Buddha," he said, "I will see the child." This boy was named Râhula, and we hear of him afterward as one among the followers of the saint.

See Spence Hardy, *Eastern Monachism*, p. 3; also Bishop Bigandet's *Legend of Gaudama*, pp. 53-57.

his person, henceforth without use for him. The horse Kantaka, born upon the same moment with Sâkya, we read, was so strongly attached to his master that he shed tears upon the separation,* and some accounts have it that his heart burst and he died on the spot.† A monument was afterward erected at the place where the coachman turned back, and Hiouen Thsang, the Chinese pilgrim, in the seventh century of our era, reports that he found it yet standing. Gautama is said to have been about twenty-nine years old at the time of this Hegira.‡

Soon as the escape was discovered, the palace was all in commotion. Swift messengers were sent in every direction, with strict orders at every hazard to bring back the prince. But they did not find him. Some of them met Tchandaka, who told them of the circumstances of the flight, and earnestly protested that his master would never be brought back alive. It remained but to return and report all at the court. Gopâ was filled with deepest sorrow, for, somewhat prepared as she had been for this departure,

---

* This also is represented in the sculptures referred to. See Fergusson, *Tree and Serpent Worship*, pl. lix.

† Bigandet, p. 61.

‡ Some accounts make it the twentieth or twenty-first year, but the nearly unanimous testimony is for the age given above.

it came as a shock to her that no most kindly consolements could relieve.

Gautama, left alone, set to work now to prepare himself for his undertaking. With his sword he cut off the long locks he had worn as symbol of his caste, and threw them to the wind. His garments, rich, of the finest silk of Benares, he exchanged with a hunter whom he met, for his single garment made of a stag's skin of yellow color. The hunter accepted the trade with a measure of embarrasment, for he perceived readily that he was dealing with some very superior person. The prince sought and was kindly received by the Brahmans, with whom and their adherents the forests seem to have been filled. Near the city of Vaisâlî * he found Arâta Kâlâma, a Brahman of great repute, who had about him three hundred disciples. The arrival of this young man, with his extraordinary antecedents, caused great attention. He was of surpassing beauty of person, and when he spoke, his words were wisdom. Kâlâma was struck by his superiority, and though he had applied for admission as a pupil, the master besought him to remain as colleague, sharing

* Vaisâlî, a few leagues north of Patna of the present day. According to Major Cunningham the ruins are still to be seen.—*The Bhilsa Topes*, p. 29.

with him the work of instruction. But the thoughtful youth did not find here what satisfied his need. Frankly he said, "This doctrine conducts not to the true deliverance. But," he added, with himself, "by completing it, since it inculcates the subjugation of the senses, I may come to the final liberation. But it needs study, patient, continuous labor to perfect it."

From Vaisâlî he went to Râjagriha,* the capital of Mâgadha, the present Behar. The story of his extraordinary appearance and character had preceded him, and the multitude, struck with the self-abnegation and personal beauty, filled all the streets as he passed. Business was suspended, for, that day, the legend tells us, "they ceased from their buying and their selling, and even from the drinking of liquors and of wine, to view the noble mendicant that was asking alms." The king Bimbisâra, who was of about the same age, and between whose father and Suddhodana there had always been an intimate friendship, observed him closely, visited him in his retreat, and "charmed with his discourse, at once so exalted and so simple, his magnanimity and his integrity," became his fast friend and protector, and afterward joined the congregation. But his most

---

* Râjagriha, about forty miles south-east of Patna, and sixteen miles south-west of Behar (the town).

flattering offers could not tempt the young devotee to remain; he had other work to do, and so he retired into deep solitudes, far from the observation and noise of the crowd.

There was in the neighborhood of Râjagriha a Brahman still more celebrated than he of Vaisâlî, Rudraka by name. He had a reputation unequaled as a teacher, both among the vulgar and the learned, and held about him a school of seven hundred disciples. Gautama sought him, asking admission as a pupil. But Rudraka, after a little acquaintance, offered, as had Arâta, to give him equal place with himself. "Together," said he, "let us teach our doctrine to this multitude." But neither here could he remain. "Friend," said Gautama, "this road leads not to indifference toward the objects of this world, leads not to conquest, serenity, perfect wisdom, leads not to Nirvâna." He withdrew, and five of his fellow pupils followed him.

In the forests of Uruvilvâ* they remained, practicing together for years the severest Brahmanic austerities. Gautama welcomed in this time, it is said, tests and trials that would have appalled the gods. What conflicts he sustained, battles with the most

---

* Uruvilvâ was a village on the banks of the present Nilajan, a tributary of the Phalgu river.

formidable demons! They tried their worst upon him, and in every instance were vanquished; broken and discomfited, were driven back to their haunts. In Oriental fashion we are told of these conflicts, personal ones with demons. In the midst of his severe penances, one day, Mâyâdêvî, alarmed for the life of her son, left Tushita, the heavenly abode, and came down to implore him to cease from this excessive self-mortification. He consoles his mother, but yields not. Then Mâra, the Evil One, essays to overcome him, and approaches with soft words of flattery. "Dear one, it is necessary to live, in order that you should perform the things you desire for mankind. The work of life ought to be done without pain. Already thou art attenuated; thy youthful bloom is faded, thou art drawing near to the grave. Gain not thy possession at too great cost. The victory over the spirit is hard, very hard to attain."

The young ascetic answers, "Pâpîyân, thou ally of whatever is delirious and insane, hither art thou come to assail and seduce me? Know that the end of life is death, inevitable. I shall not seek to escape it. Armed with courage and with wisdom, there is no creature in the world that can move me. Demon, soon shall I gain the conquest over thee. The desires are thy first soldiers, ennui the next, then the passions, love of ease, fear, anger, ambition, false fame, self-praise, censoriousness, — these are thy black hosts. Thy soldiers reduce the gods as the world of men. But I will destroy them by wisdom."

Then he did battle with these demons, fought in the wilderness and overcame, and Mâra, humiliated and ashamed, for the time withdrew. Ere long, however, the sons of the gods came to make an attack upon him still more formidable. He was fasting severely, and his very life was passing away. They offered to infuse nourishment through the pores of his skin, and enable him to show the peasants the miracle of a man, sustained in good vigor, who took no food. He rejected with scorn and indignation the proffer. "Yes, verily, I might show the peasants such a spectacle, and they might believe that Sramana eats not at all, all the while being secretly nourished in this manner by the sons of the gods, but it were on my part a huge lie. Nay, indeed!" And so, in his own dialect, this son of man also in the wilderness, declares, "Get thee behind me, Satan. Man shall not live by bread alone, but by every word that proceedeth from the mouth of God."

Other conflicts remained; before attaining Bôdhi, the highest wisdom and possession, he must achieve still more conquests. He challenged the prince of the infernal regions, with all his black hosts, to combat. Sending from a point between his eyebrows (a little tuft of hair that was one of the thirty-two signs upon him at birth), a beam of light that pierced and made to tremble all the depths of hell, he roused Pâpîyân, who, alarmed for his kingdom, summoned all his forces together. A council of war was held. Some were for yielding, at least, making no attempt, foreseeing certain defeat. Others were for every adventure desperation could make, believing in victory. This counsel prevailed. Four *corps d'armée* there were, hideous and frightful beyond description. The demons changed their visage in a hundred million ways, their hands and their feet were intertwined with ten thousand serpents, they carried swords, bows, pikes, javelins, hatchets, clubs, pestles, and all the weapons known to that time, thunderbolts included; their heads were lurid with flame; belly, feet, hands of most disgusting aspect; their teeth projected in tusks, the tongue swollen and hanging from the mouth; their eyes shot fire like those of the poisonous black serpent.

With these dire hosts came the assault upon the single solitary soul. But in vain; utterly impotent and baffled they were. The pikes, javelins, and the huge rocks even, that they hurled at him, *transmuted* *to flowers, and gathered in garlands about his head.* Pâpîyân made other attempts. Foiled in violence, he tried the arts of persuasion, sent his daughters, the beautiful Apsaras, to tempt Bôdhisattva,* exhibiting to him the thirty-two kinds of bewitchment known to women. They sang and they danced before him, and plied him with all imaginable fascinations and seductive charms, but they were alike unsuccessful as their brothers had been. Nay, they were themselves overcome, and out of compelled respect and esteem, broke forth in songs of praise to that virtue which was too high that their art could touch. Pâpîyân puts forth once more a last desperate attempt, but is disappointed and stung, to see his very sons, who had been most eager for the conflict, turned to adore and worship Gautama. In his despair he smote upon his breast and uttered groans; retiring by himself, he traced with his arrow upon the ground, "My kingdom is departed."† Such is the legend, wrought in all the extravagance of Oriental imagination, and yet it is nowise difficult to see the groundwork of severe truth that lay at the bottom.

---

* Bôdhisattva, a general term applied to characterize any one who is aspiring and striving after the Buddhahood — state of superior wisdom and liberation.

† The scene of the temptation also is depicted on the northern gateway of the temple at Sanchi, middle beam. See Fergusscn as as above, frontispiece.

But we have anticipated a little. Before Gautama had passed all these conflicts, he had renounced the ascetic practices of the Brahmans, satisfied that they afforded not the vaunted road to deliverance, and returned to a more free and normal life. "As the man," he somewhere says, "who would discourse sweet music, must tune the strings of his instrument to the medium point of tension, so he who would arrive at the condition of Buddha must exercise himself in a medium course of discipline." This scandalized the five friends who had followed him from Râjagriha, and they forsook him in deep displeasure. He was left alone, and by himself he commenced to elaborate with patient care the thought which to his mind was to be the life of the world.

He had learned himself, he had vanquished his adversaries, he knew now somewhat of the foes he he was to meet, and his power to resist them. But had he got distinct view of the high wisdom? Did he see the *way* so clearly that he could make it plain to others? He recalled the experiences of his childhood, the splendid visions that had come to him in early years in that garden of his father's under the bamboo tree. Would his thought, ripened by reflection, fulfil and realize these high promises? Could the day-dream become a reality? After days and weeks spent in deep, rapt thought, he was able to say, Yes. He had found the way, had seen the vision of life—the way, he describes it, "of the sacrifice of sense, the way which shows the path of deliverance, leads to the possession of universal knowledge, the way of remembrance and of clear judgment, softening old age and death, calm, without anxiety, free from all fear, and bringing to the home of Nirvâna." Here he had become as he deemed, Buddha, the illuminated, fully conscious, perfectly emancipate and free. An entire day and night, it is said, he sat under the Bôdhi tree, and it had become the last watch, the first gleam of the day-dawn, when the vision came, "he was clothed with the quality of perfect wisdom, he attained the triple science." All nature at this moment testified her joy.* "All the flower-trees in the various sakwalas (systems of worlds) put forth blossoms; and to the same extent the fruit-trees became laden with fruit. On the trunks and branches there were lotus-flowers, whilst garlands were suspended from the sky. The rocks were rent, and upon them flowers appeared, in ranges of seven, one above the other. The Lôkântarika hills, 80,000 miles in extent, in all these sakwalas, were illuminated by a more brilliant light than could have been made by seven suns. The waters of the great ocean, 840,000 miles deep, became fresh. The streams of the rivers were arrested. The blind from birth saw, the deaf heard, the lame walked, and the bound prisoner was set free." *

The place where he was visited with this high experience is celebrated in the Buddhistic annals; it was called Bodhimanda—the seat of intelligence. The tree under which Gautama was sitting became historic, and the faithful in after ages did not fail to gather about it, and pay there a most devout worship. In the year 632 of our era, Hiouen Thsang, the Chinese pilgrim, found the tree, or at least what was reputed to be it, still standing. It was protected by a circle of brick wall, and approached by gates opening on the east, south and west. "Its trunk was of creamy white, its leaves green and glossy, and according to the information given our traveler they never fell, either in autumn or winter. Only on the anniversary-day of the Nirvâna (death) of Buddha they fall all at once, to be reproduced the next day more beautiful than before. Each year, on that same day, the kings, ministers, magistrates, etc., gather about it, shower it with milk, illumine with lamps, scatter flowers about it, and carry away the leaves that have fallen." †

---

* Hardy's *Legends and Theories of the Buddhists*, pp. 139, 140. See also Bigandet's *Legend*, etc., pp. 90, 91.

† St. Hilaire's *Bouddha*, pp. 29, 30.

There was still one ground on which Buddha felt hesitation. Sure as he was of himself, clear as was his own view of the way, he had doubt whether this high doctrine could be commended by him so it should be accepted. "It is subtle and deep, beyond the reach of the understanding, open only to wise souls; is in conflict with all the world. How will it be received? Men will not apprehend it. It may only be rejected, and I be mocked. Hardly should I expose myself to their insults, and be my own victim." Three times he was on the point of yielding, taking in view the easily possible—nay, as seemed, the very probable consequences of his standing forth as a public teacher. But consideration of the needs of men prevailed, and banished every hesitation.

"Three classes of men," he said within himself, "one finds, very much as when one sits beside a tank and notes the water-lilies growing in it; he sees some below the surface, others with heads raised quite above it, and others still just on the surface. So all mankind are of these three—the sunken, the hopelessly bad, the confirmedly virtuous, and the undecided, the wavering. The first I may not help, the second are strong, and do not need me, but the third—shall I leave them to perish? Perhaps my word will save them, or some of them." Infinite compassion moved him, and he resolved to devote himself henceforth, without thought of anything personal to himself, to the redemption of man.

His first idea was that he would seek his old masters at Vaisâlî and Râjagriha, both of whom he remembered with tender affection. But it was a long while since he parted from them, and in the interval they had passed away. Could he have been earlier, he said with himself, sorrowfully, he might have helped these old friends; now, alas! it was too late. His next thought was of the five disciples who had left him, and he resolved to seek them. They were all young men of a generous strain; might be they would hear the law. They were at Vârânasi (Benares), and he must needs cross the Ganges. The river was at this time high and very rapid, and he found some difficulty in getting ferried over, for he had no money to pay with. King Bimbisâra, learning of the circumstance, afterwards abolished all charge for ferriage to devotees.

The five saw him approaching, and all their old remembrance of the offense he gave them came up. They agreed among themselves that they would have no conversation with him, would offer him no seat, have nothing to do with him. But the presence of their old master disarmed them, they sat uneasy, and instinctively were constrained to rise and honor him.

They gave him a mat, and water for his feet, and addressed him, "Ayushmat (Master) Gautama, welcome! Pray sit down upon the mat. Sire, have you risen beyond human law, and attained clear vision of the sublime science?" "Call me not Ayushmat," he responded. "Long time have I remained without profit to you. I have not given you help or any benefit. Yes, I have arrived at clear vision of immortality, have seen the way that guides thither. Come, let me teach you the Law. Your spirits shall be delivered by the destruction of all your faults, and clear knowledge of yourselves; you shall make an end of births, and arrive at supreme possession." Then pleasantly he recalled to them the language, not kindly, they had indulged in as they saw him coming. Ashamed and confused they confessed their sins, and gladly embraced him as their teacher and the guide of the world. The interview, we are told, on this first meeting was long, lasted to the latest watch of the night, and Buddha unfolded to them freely his doctrine. It was the enthusiasm of the teacher freshly entered upon his work; of the learner, hearing for the first time the quickening word.

Benares was, as it still is, a distinguished seat and radiating center of the Brahmanical doctrine. Here was good missionary ground, and the young prophet improved it well. As the story reads, here he turned, for the first time, the wheel of the law. The preaching was earnest and startling, and for a time commanded all ears. All the classes, from Brahman to Kandâla, gathered to hear it. As usual, men blessed and cursed. Some accepted gladly, others turned away with scorn and offense. The old charge of madness was repeated. They said, "The son of the king has lost his reason." The legends are mostly silent concerning this history, and of others how much, in what they profess to give, is authentic we cannot know.

The first conversion after that of the five, one relation tells us, was of a young layman, son of a very wealthy citizen of Benares. This youth, wearied and sick with the round of luxuries and sensuous pleasures that were provided for him, stole away by night from his home and sought the feet of the saint, heard the law, and gladly accepted. The father, going all about in search of his son, came erewhile into the same presence, and he too was won. "O, illustrious master," he exclaimed, "your doctrine is a most excellent one; when you preach it you do like one who replaces on its base an upset cup; like one who brings to light precious things that had hitherto remained in darkness; one who opens the mind's eyes that they may see the pure truth." Invited to the house of the father, Buddha gained the mother and the wife of the young man. Next four young men, then fifty, we are told, of the best in the city, friends and companions of this youth, moved by his example, came in and gave up their lives to religion. "All these," as one of the legends in Chinese puts it, "were but instances of the virtue of the overflowing streams of the heavenly dew (divine grace), and the enlightening power of the mani gem (divine wisdom)."

The discipleship so numerous, counting now more than sixty, Buddha must erewhile send these men forth to evangelize. The good news was for all the world; let them hasten to preach it to every creature. "Let us part with each other," the legend reports him as saying, "and proceed in various and opposite directions. Go ye now, and preach the most excellent law, expounding every point thereof, and unfolding it with care. Explain the beginning and middle and end of the law to *all men without exception.* You will meet, doubtless, with a great number of mortals, not as yet hopelessly given up to their passions, who will avail themselves of your preaching for reconquering their hitherto forfeited liberty, and freeing themselves from the thralldom of passions." This was the first sending forth of the apostles, of which history has preserved us any record. The mission, as we see, was to humanity.

Such work was accomplished not without opposition. There were heart-burnings, jealousies, ill reports, and at length plots, machinations against him, so that at times he was in imminent peril of his life. The authors and instigators, as we should naturally know, were the Brahmans. They instantly saw how this reform would bear upon their exclusive claims and position, and they left no means untried to crush it in its incipiency. Here was a man that met them on their own ground, and worsted them; that challenged them to public debate, and was too much for them, put them to shame, and what could be done with him but to silence his voice? Mild as he was, Buddha did not spare them; he exposed their tricks and impostures, and set the brand upon them deep, of hypocrites and charlatans. Probably to the fact of the more pacific or less violent temper of the Indian blood we owe it that here again was not enacted such tragedy as that of the crucifixion at Jerusalem, or the poisoning at Athens.

Leaving Benares the story conducts him to the forest of Uruvilvâ, where he wrought many conversions — the legend says one thousand, including the distinguished teacher Kâsyapa — and erewhile to Râjagriha. King Bimbasâra had invited him hither. His reception was very hospitable, and in this neighborhood, Mâgadha, and in Kôsalâ, whose capital was

Srâvastî, and king, Prasênajit, very friendly to Buddha, he seems to have spent thenceforth a large part of his life. One of his favorite resorts was a high hill, called the Vulture Peak, from a fancied resemblance to that bird, overlooking Râjagriha; it afforded magnificent views, as also fine shade and fountains. Some of his most famous discourses are marked as having been delivered here. Hard by was the garden or grove of Kalantaka, which a rich merchant of the city presented him, having built upon it a superb monastery, for the use of the disciples. Here were converted Sâriputra, Kâtyâyana and Maudgalyâyana, names eminently distinguished in the subsequent history. Another grove, Nâlanda, is mentioned, a little farther distant from the city, which became very celebrated in this connection. Hiouen Thsang saw here, at the time of his visit, immense monasteries, the finest, he tells us, in all India, and ten thousand monks dwelling in them, all maintained at the public expense.

But in Kôsala, which was north of the Ganges, Buddha spent more time than in Mâgadha. King Prasênajit invited him to his capital, and became a disciple. Here also, near the city, was a grove that became famous, one that Anâtha Pindika, a minister of the king, long-time distinguished for his boundless beneficence to the poor and orphaned, purchased and presented to him. He also erected upon it a monastery, and here, it is said, that for twenty-three years Buddha made his principal residence, teaching all that came. Prajâpati, his aunt, embraced the faith here, and became the first of the female Buddhist devotees. A great innovation it was upon the old-time usage, to admit females to monastic orders, and Ananda, his cousin, is said to have been largely instrumental in effecting it.

After a separation of twelve years, Buddha saw again his father and kindred of Kapilavastu. He had attained the illumination and deliverance, and the time for the fulfillment of the prophecy was come. The father, grieved much at the withdrawal of his son, sent many messengers, successively, to communicate with him, but all were so charmed by his person and speech that they forgot to return. At length he sent one of his ministers, Tcharka. He, like the rest, was won, but returned, to tell the king what he had seen, and announced the contemplated visit. The king anticipated, and came to see his son. What effect this had upon the father we know not, but we are told that Buddha soon after went to Kapilavastu, and all the Sâkyas, hearing him, embraced the faith. Among them was his son, Râhula. And Gopâ, or, as some say, Yasôdharâ, who, in sympathy, had followed her husband all the while since his departure, adopting, fast as she learned of them, his diet and his plain style of dress—she and five hundred other women of rank became converts and assumed the monastic robe.

The scene of his activity must have been wider than the comparatively narrow domain we have mentioned. We hear of him on the banks of the Indus—the scene of his feeding a hungry tigress with his own arm is laid here, and Hiouen Thsang, eleven hundred years later, found the grass, he tells us, still red with the blood that flowed,—and there was probably little of Northern India that he did not at some time visit. Three several times, the Singhalese annals tell us, he visited their island, and he left there in two places the prints of his sacred feet. But the legends are very fragmentary and uncertain here, long stretches of years are left entirely blank, and much that is said of the wide journeyings, etc., may quite likely be a later addition. We have enough to show that it was a very busy life, intensely devoted to the word and works of kindliness and mercy. Probably a portion of those years over which the veil of silence hangs was spent in withdrawal, hiding away from the reach of those enemies that sought his blood.

We select from among the incidents related, a few, which, whether authentic or not, have a verisimilitude and are not unworthy of record. King Suddhodana, already far advanced in years, was seized with a violent distemper, that gave him no rest, by day or by night. He felt strong, irrepressible desire once more to see his son. Buddha, while in the early morning, as was his wont, viewing the condition of all beings, and devising in his compassionate heart what might be done for them, saw the condition of his father, and he hastened, traveling, as did Abaris the Hyperborean, through the air, to his side. By skillful appliances he healed the disease, but, announcing to Suddhodana that in seven days he must die, expounded to him the law. Suddhodana saw, believed and found repose. "Rocking himself in the bosom of these comforting truths," he spent happily the few days he had yet to live. On the last day, in presence of all his royal attendants, he asked pardon for all the offenses he had committed in thought, word or deed, and expired in the arms of his son, in the ninety-seventh year of his age. Buddha consoled the wife, Prajâpati, by reminding of the transience of all earthly, the inevitable separation that comes to every one, and the home of possession to which the four paths lead.

In the fields one day he met a Brahman, who was a farmer, with bullocks, plough, seed, etc. He was tilling and planting for the future harvest.

Entering into conversation with him upon his work, and the instruments employed in the performance, he hinted that he himself was also a husbandman, cultivating a domain, and having need of and using all the apparatus found with the best furnished farmer. The Brahman, somewhat suprised and puzzled, Buddha explains to him what in this husbandry is seed, what the plough, the reins for guiding, the bullocks, etc. "The bullocks have to work hard to complete the task of tillage. So the sage has to struggle hard to till perfectly and cultivate thoroughly the soil of his own being, and reach the happy state of Nirvâna." The worker in the field of earth is sometimes disappointed, sometimes feels the pangs of hunger. But the worker in the field of wisdom, he says, knows no failure, and is exempt from all suffering and sorrow. He eats the fruit of his labor, and is fully satisfied when he beholds Nirvâna.

A Brahman and his wife, in one of the towns he visited, were very friendly, proffered him hospitality and sought his blessing. During many existences, they said, we have always been happily united. Not an unpleasant word has ever passed between us. We pray that in our coming existence the same love and affection may ever unite us together. Their request was granted; in presence of a large assembly Buddha pronounced them blessed, happy among all men and women. A poor weaver's daughter, intensely desirous to hear the teacher, stops on her way to the loom, quill and yarn in her hand, and sits down timidly behind the furthermost rank of the congregation. The saint sees her, and calls her forward, catechises, instructs and blesses her, extolling her thoughtful wisdom and earnest love for the true.

In a forest of Kôsala dwelt a famous robber and murderer, the terror of the neighborhood. Many had fallen victims, and the king was powerless to afford protection against him. Buddha, coming that way, went, despite all remonstrances, boldly to his den. Ugalimala, very wroth, set out instantly to slay him. But the saint, by his perfect self-possession, his kindliness, benignity and commanding presence disarmed, subdued the hard man, won him to the law, and brought him in a disciple. Henceforth he lived worthily and rose to the attainment of a Rahan.

Dêvadatta, a cousin, and for a time a disciple of Buddha, with the full countenance of King Ajâtasatru, hired thirty bowmen to take his life. Practiced ruffians, they were nothing loth, rather were eager for the deed. But just as they were about to put it into execution, they were restrained, incapacitated, "they felt themselves overawed by the presence of Buddha." Instead of his murderers they became worshipers, "fell at his feet, craved pardon, listened to his preaching, and were converted." At another time an elephant, infuriated, maddened by liquor that had been forced down his throat, was set upon him as he was quietly walking in the street. But the elephant, as he came into his presence, far from doing him injury, stood for a while, then knelt before him.* Such relations may be in a degree fabulous, yet they rest in a groundwork of severe truth; the writer drew from ideals, was veracious. It is natural to believe in the greatness of the soul, to think it will sometimes bear itself superior to all, work every conquest; nay, it is sometimes found so.

Near the close of his life — he was already advanced in years — a very tragic fortune befell his family and native city. A neighboring king, for some fancied offense, marched against it, captured it and put all the inhabitants to the sword. Sâkya, who had in vain attempted to calm this vindictive ruler, and dissuade him from his purpose of blood, remained, as it is related, in the neighborhood of the unhappy city, and heard distinctly the wild din of the battle and the wail of the dying. After Virûdhaka's (the king's) departure he repaired in the night-time alone to the city, and strolled through its desolate and

---

Bigandet, pp. 249, 250.

corpse-covered streets. In that charming garden, near Suddhodana's palace, where in his childhood he had spent days together, he heard only death-groans, and saw by the starlight naked, mutilated bodies, members and trunks, scattered promiscuously about. Many of the victims were already dead, some in the last struggle. "He went from one to another, ministered to them of his deep sympathy, and comforted them in the assurance of the blessed beyond." *

About forty-five years he had spent in unremitting self-denial and toil, his courage never failing, his zeal never for an instant growing cold, when the time for his departure had come. He was nearly eighty years old. He was returning from Râjagriha, towards Kôsala, accompanied by Ananda, his cousin, and a large crowd of disciples. Standing upon a square stone, on the bank of the Ganges, he looked back towards Râjagriha, and remarked, with deep emotion, "Never again shall I see that city or the Throne of Diamond"—this last being the place where he wrought his great victory and attained the Buddhahood. A like touching adieu he bade to Vaisâlî. He had not quite reached the city of Kusinagâra †

* Koeppen's *Buddha*, I., pp. 113, 114.

† Lying a little more than one hundred miles northwest of the present Patna.

— city of Kusa grass — when he felt that the end was at hand. He requested Ananda to prepare a place for him in a forest of Sâla trees (*shorea robusta*) hard by. Pointing out two tall trees on the edge of the wood, he directed that the couch should be laid between them. Though the distance was short he made it only with great embarrassment, was compelled to rest twenty-five times on the way. Beneath these trees he spent his last hours, busily engaged upon the themes that had occupied his life. "The sun and moon shall decay; what, then, is the sparkle of the glow-worm? Therefore he exhorted them to strive after the imperishable body, to cast away the unreal." All the watches of the night he employed in kindly counsel to his friends, in earnest preaching to the Malla princes and the Brahman Subhadra, whom he converted there; at the break of day he passed away. This occurred, according to the most probable determination, about 477 B. C.*

While he was reclining on the couch, the account is that the two Sâla trees became loaded with fragrant blossoms, which gently dropped above and all around his person, so almost to cover it. Not only these, but all in the forest, and in ten thousand worlds,

* The Ceylonese Buddhists fix the time at 543 B. C. Practically the difference is of but little moment. Bunsen, on what authority does not appear, makes his death to have occurred in the fifty-sixth year of his age.

went likewise into bloom. As the end approached, the blood of the Palâsa flower poured forth, and at the moment of the death a fearful earthquake occurred, that shook the whole world; sun and moon were darkened, meteors flashed abroad, and finest dirge music, sounding from the skies, filled the air.*

Ananda had inquired what ceremonies were to be performed after his demise. "Be not much concerned about what shall remain of me after my Nirvâna," was the reply, "rather be earnest to practice the works that lead to perfection. Put on those inward dispositions that will enable you to reach the undisturbed rest of Nirvâna." "Believe not," he says again, "that when I shall have disappeared from existence and be no longer with you, Buddha has left you and ceased to dwell among you. *The law contained in those sacred instructions which I have given shall be your teacher. By means of the doctrines which I have delivered to you, I will continue to remain amongst you.*" † Obedience, he insists, is greater than sacrifice. The Nagas,

---

* Beal's *Catena*, p. 137. Bigandet, *Legend*, etc., p. 323. Koeppen, I., p. 115.

† In one of the Sûtras of the Prajna Pâramitâ class in the Chinese, on "the mystical body of Tathâgata, without any distinct characteristic," we find this: "He who looks for me, *i. e.*, for the true Tathâgata, through any material form, or seeks me through any audible sound, that man has entered on an erroneous course, and shall never behold Tathâgata.—Beal's *Catena*, p. 277.

Galongs and Nats, all coming from their respecttive seats in the other worlds, showered flowers and perfumes, like dew, over and about his person. He said to Ananda, "The man or woman who practices the excellent works leading to perfect happiness—these are the persons that render me a true homage and present to me a most agreeable offering. The observance of the law alone entitles to the right of belonging to my religion." To Ananda, who was the beloved disciple, the John of this band, he predicts something of his future, the attraction he shall exercise, the warm, glowing love he shall win. "Ananda is graceful and full of amiability amidst all other Rahans. He has heard and seen much, he shines in the midst of the assembly. Rahans will come from a distance, on hearing all that is said of his graces, to see and admire him; and all will agree in saying that what they observe surpasses all that they had heard." "Enraptured at the flow of his tender, touching and heart-moving eloquence, visitors shall eagerly listen to him; they will experience sadness only when his silence shall deprive them of that food their mind and heart were feasting on."

Whatever may have been the wishes of the saint—and it would seem that he would have made very little account of the lifeless, perishing body—the grandest obsequies followed upon his death. They were after the manner appointed for the Chakravarttin kings, to whom, by descent, he reputedly belonged. On the eighth day the body was burned. At first the flames refused to do their office, but when Kâsyapa had honored the feet of the dead, the "flame of contemplation" burst forth from the breast, and consumed the entire corpse. The bones were of pearly whiteness, and they exhaled a fragrant odor, sweet as the breath of heaven. After hot disputes, which the history tells us, but for the remembrance of the amity and tender spirit of affection which the Master had taught, would have been bloody, these relics were divided into eight portions, and distributed to as many groups of friends, not omitting the Sâkyas. Immense topes were afterwards erected over the several places where they lay, but in the time of King Asoka, about 250 B. C., they were gathered together again, redistributed, and sent abroad over the whole of India.

We have some particulars of the person of this saint. He was not only a model of wisdom, sanctity, high character, but also of physical beauty. In the crown, we are told, his head rose very high, the hair was curly, and of deep black, the forehead broad and smooth, "the eye-lashes like those of a heifer," and the eyes jet black. "His brows were arched like the rainbow, his eyes ribbed like the leaf of the lotus." The teeth, in number forty, were regular, and of pearly whiteness. Every limb, every feature, down to the lines of the hand, fingers, finger-nails, etc., was modeled after the standard of perfect beauty, according to the Indian ideal, and all the details are carefully given. A likeness, accurate to the life, done in sandal-wood, is said to have been executed by one of the disciples, and to have served as the model of all the statues and portraits found in the North, wherever the faith penetrated. Another, a portrait upon canvas, made for King Bimbasâra, as a present to a neighboring prince, is ascribed, in the outline at least, to Buddha himself. How far the representations we now have were modeled upon these ancient pictures, supposing them to have existed, no one, of course, can tell. The face, in such as we have seen, bears a marked expression of fineness, of sweetness, illumination and beauty.*

* The sources whence we have drawn, in preparing this sketch, are in good part indicated above. We name them together here: Barthelemy St. Hilaire's *Le Bouddha et Sa Religion.* Troisieme Edition, Paris, 1866. C. F. Koeppen, *Die Religion des Buddha, und ihre Entstehung*, Berlin, 1857, 1859. Eugene Burnouf's *Introduction a la Histoiré du Buddhisme Indien*, Paris, 1844. S. Beal's *Catena of Buddhist Scriptures, from the Chinese;* London, 1871. Spence Hardy's *Eastern Monachism*, London, 1860. The same, *Legends and Theories of the Buddhists*, London, 1866. Wasseljew's *Buddhismus, seine Dogmen, Geschichte und Literatur*, St. Petersburg, 1860; and last, but not least, Bishop Bigandet's *Life or Legend of Gaudama*, Rangoon, 1866. The agreement in the accounts preserved among the Northern

Buddhists and the Southern respectively is singularly close, and shows clearly that they have all guarded with scrupulous care their sacred records, in this regard, from essential change since their separation, and gives good ground to believe that we have them now in all important respects, as they were when first committed to writing. How soon this was done we do not know, but there is evidence that the Salita Vistara, the chief book of this kind among the Northern Buddhists, and rendered early into Chinese, Thibetan, etc., is of a date previous to the Christian era. See Max Müller, *Chips*, I., p. 259.

In Beal's *Catena*, pp. 130–142, is a remarkable statement of the legend, made by Wong-Puh, in the seventh century, who drew, as he says, from the old records. It is in aphorisms, and written in the style that was common in the schools at an early date.

II.

THE EFFECT.

THE success that attended the preaching of this new faith was wonderful. Preaching itself was a novelty, for Burnouf says that, so far as he finds, it was a thing unheard of in India before.* Even during the life-time of its founder, his doctrine must have obtained a considerable prevalence, slow at first, doubtless, making its conquests at the hardest, but gaining each year, until at length it became broadspread over the country. It supplanted Brahmanism largely on its own soil. We have no means of knowing what its numerical strength then was, but the following must have been large.† The old was effete, gone utterly to decay, and the preaching of salvation by method so simple, natural, pure and enforced by life, and earnestness so devoted and transparent, could

* *Introd.* p. 194.

† The number reported by the early Buddhists as converted directly by Buddha himself is 1,250.—Wasseljew, p. 26.

not fail to draw followers.* It brought quickening regeneration in the midst of prevailing death. It was a simple word of repentance and obedience, of high consecration and pure living, practical and intelligible, so far as the ethereal and transcendent truths that dwell in light inaccessible, can be brought to the understanding. There was no ceremonial, no elaborate scheme of expiation and deliverance. The handwriting of ordinances was blotted out, the immense structures broken down which priestly device had thrown about the soul to hedge it out from God. What a sense of relief it must have brought to many a poor, sick, weary and harrassed one, those may somewhat imagine who have known the like in their own experience.

Buddha proclaimed the equality of all, no distinction of blood or caste; all were alike before the law. "The Brahman is born of a woman, so is the Kandâla. Can you see any cause that should make the one noble and the other vile? The Brahman, when he dies, becomes a loathsome object, as does any one of a lower caste; where, then, is the difference?" "My law is a law of grace for all." "As

* "If there is one broad fact that comes out from the legends of every kind, it is that Indian society was most deeply corrupt at the time when Buddha appeared there."—St. Hilaire, p. 95. To the same effect, Koeppen, I., p. 56.

the four rivers which flow into the Ganges, lose their names so soon as they mingle their waters with the sacred stream, so those who believe in Buddha cease to be Brahmans, Kshatriyas, Vaisyas and Sûdras."

"Since the doctrine which I proclaim is altogether pure, it makes no distinction between high and low, rich and poor. Like water it is, which washes and purifies all alike. It is like the sky, for it has room for all, men, women, boys, girls, rich and poor." *

How revolutionary it must have been, in a country ridden as no country ever was before or since, with the oppressions of caste! He was himself a model of all the virtues and benignities he taught, and enforced every word with such personal consecration and love as touched deeply the heart.

The wave of this influence was not soon spent. For the first time, so far as any records show us, the soul of humanity was kindled, the missionary spirit,

* "He addressed himself to all classes; nay, he addressed himself to the poor and degraded, rather than to the rich and the high."—M. Müller, *Chips*, II., p. 343. "The whole proletary of India you would see in the assemblage of our reformer; Sûdras and Kandâlas, barbers and scavengers, bankrupts, the imbecile, forsaken, aged, beggars and cripples, worn-out courtesans, outcast girls, that knew no couch but the dung-hill; even thieves and highwaymen, murderers — in a word, all the wretched and unfortunate, eagerly seek him, to gain through him deliverance from their burdens."—Koeppen, I., p. 132.

the desire to carry the new word to all nations, was aroused. As early as the date of the third Council, say perhaps 308 years before Christ, we hear of extended missionary enterprises into foreign countries, into Cashmire on the north, beyond the Himâlas to Thibet, and perhaps China, and into Ceylon and Farther India. Indeed there are accounts of some of this work done far earlier, but how far they are trustworthy it is not possible now to decide.* The new religion had its poets. The soul was touched to rhythm, and the fine thought found fine utterance in the music of song. This was sure to come. The annals are mostly vacant, but we find mention made of a lyric poet, Pârsva, in the reign of King Kanishka (a little before the Christian era), who did very much to popularize Buddhism, celebrating it in odes that were presently in the mouths of all. Others also are named; two laymen, brothers in Magadha, whose hymns are still preserved, or profess to be, in one of the sacred collections (the Tanjur) of Thibet.† Fahian, a Chinese pilgrim in the fourth century, found Buddhism prevalent in the Cabul countries west of the Indus. In the reign of Ming-ti, emperor A. D.

---

* See the substance of them in Wasseljew, pp. 42–44. But see also Koeppen. I., pp. 144, 188.

† Wasseljew, pp. 52, 53.

65, it gained public recognition as the third among the state religions of China, and it has maintained a strong hold there to this day, being professed in a sort by the lower classes of the people at large. In the seventh century there were not less than 3,716 Buddhistic monasteries there, and at the present time, in Peking and its environs alone, there are 5,000 temples and 80,000 monks. The number of priests in the empire is reported at over 1,000,000. From China it was carried in the fifth century to Corea, and in the sixth to Japan. Among the Tartar tribes it must have been propagated at least a century or two before our era. On the west at an early day it penetrated into Persia proper, but was repressed and driven back into Cabul by the relentless power of the Sassanidae. Then soon came the Mohammedan persecutions, which lasted for centuries, and extended over all of Central Asia, as far as the banks of the Lob Nor. In these calamities, doubtless, very many literary documents of great value, touching the religion and its history, perished.* Like Christianity, Buddhism was first itself when transplanted to foreign soil; it achieved its great conquests among those of different nationality, blood and civilization, from the people with whom it had its birth.

---

* Wasseljew, pp. 79, 80. Also Koeppen, II., p. 34.

A son of King Asoka, Mahinda, is said, with his sister, to have been sent to Ceylon,* and a very wonderful account of the history of the planting of the faith in that island is contained in one of the old Singhalese annals.

King Dêvânampîyatissa ruled over the island. Before he ascended the throne he was greatly distinguished for wisdom and piety. On the day of his coronation all Nature testified her rejoicing; rich metals and precious stones came up of their own accord from the bowels of the earth, and spread themselves upon the surface. Pearls and other treasures, buried in the depths of the sea, rose and ranged themselves upon the shore, happy in the possession of such a prince. More marvelous still, a bamboo put forth three wonderful branches, one of silver, one covered with the most varied and beautiful flowers, and one graved with figures of the rarest animals and birds. The king, too modest to appropriate them himself, sent these choice treasures to the great Asoka. His embassadors came back, loaded with finest gifts, and charged with a message to their

---

* Maudgaliputra, head of the third Council, deputed Mahinda, with his associates, commissioning them in these words: "Establish ye, in the delightful land of Lankâ, the delightful religion of the Vanquisher."—The Singhalese Mahâvansa, quoted by Koeppen, I., p. 188, Note.

sovereign: "I have found refuge with Buddha, the Law and the Congregation; I am dedicated to the religion of the son of the Sâkyas. Come, thou sovereign of men, acknowledge in thy heart this supreme refuge, and commit to it thy salvation."

We do not know that the message received any immediate regard, but erewhile Mahinda and his sister were sent as missionaries to the island. The new faith was accepted. Dêvânampîyatissa, the Princess Annula and all the court embraced it, and the people flocked in crowds, to hear and receive. Mahinda became, as the old chronicler hath it, "the torchlight whereby the whole island was illuminated." Great memorial structures grew up, but they lacked relics, and King Asoka was applied to, to supply them. A collar-bone of Buddha was sent, which was received and provided for with all due honor.

But more than all, a branch of that sacred tree, the *Bo-tree* at Bodhimanda, was sent, cut by the hand of the king, and carefully guarded by himself in person, until it was committed to the ship that was to carry it to the island. The most remarkable prodigies occurred on the way. The vessel cut swiftly the waves, and to the distance of a league away the rough billows subsided to smooth sea before it. Flowers of five different colors bloomed around it, and music, the most sweet and luscious, filled the air. Innumerable oblations were brought by innumerable divinities, while the Nâgas tried in vain to steal away this divine tree. Sanghamittâ, the daughter of King Asoka, herself a high priestess, into whose hands this noble branch was committed for keeping, baffled all their wicked designs "by the power of her sanctity,"

Such was the story of the tree in its passage. Arrived at its destination, the capital city, Anurâdhapura, it is borne in imposing procession, to be planted in the garden of Mahâmega. Sixteen princes, clad in the most brilliant habits, are at hand to receive it, but the branch, leaving their grasp, rises aloft in the air, and stays there, glistening with a circle of light, which six luminous rays make about it. At the setting of the sun it descends again and plants itself without assistance, in the garden, where, for the space of eight days, a sheltering cloud protects it, watering it with quickening showers. Instantly then the fruits appear on the tree, and the king is thereby enabled to disseminate it over the island — this wonderful tree, Bôdhi, pledge of salvation.

A faith supported by such prodigies ought to grow, or perhaps we might better say it had already attained large dimensions that there should have been such prodigies. The hold which Buddhism gained in Ceylon has never been broken, and although much degenerated from the pure simplicity and transparent truth of its founder, it still retains many points of singular attractiveness and worth.*

It was effectually introduced into Thibet in the seventh century of our era, although it seems to have been preached there long time before, and after various fortunes — sometimes encountering the bitterest persecutions — it was at length established as the prevailing religion. Variously colored and mixed, modified by Sivaism, which it brought from India, and the Shamanism which it found on Mongolian soil, grown now to a most rigid and narrow ecclesiasticism, with its lamaseries, hierarchy, pontifical college and Grand Lama, it still retains some of the fine features of its parentage, and is reverently called by the Thibetan people "the internal religion." †

In India, the land of its birth, after various fortunes, having been installed as the state religion, by King Asoka, and sometimes favored and some-

---

* See here Hardy's *Eastern Monachism*, a book written from an orthodox Christian standpoint, by a missionary, and blind to much that ought to have been seen and appreciated; but, on the whole, pervaded by a spirit more than usually intelligent and candid.

† In three cloisters, in or near Lhassa, are at the present time 30,000 monks.—Koeppen, II., 111. These are of the yellow mantle. In the south of Thibet there is another church, of the Buddhists of the red mantle, with their Lama also, but of their number, as indeed of the number of the others, we are not informed.

times persecuted by succeeding monarchs, Buddhism was assailed and expelled by its old enemy, the Brahmanical power. This final expulsion occurred about the eleventh or twelfth century of our era.* "Let him who slays not be slain," read the decree, and the disciples of the meek Gautama were massacred and driven out by the sword.† Not a single Buddhist to-day, it is said, is to be found on the peninsula.

The influence of Buddhism upon the western world, through the intercourse that, after the conquests of Alexander, sprung up between West and East, and lasted for centuries, was neither slight nor transient.

---

* Cunningham, *Bhilsa Topes*, p. 166.

† Spence Hardy puts it in the sixth century after Christ, but this is certainly too early, for Chinese pilgrims visited India in subsequent centuries, and found the faith widely current there. "The prince Sudhanvan gave orders to put all the Buddhists in India to death." Mâdhava Achârayâ says: "The king commanded his servants to put to death the old men and the children of the Bauddhas, from the bridge of Râma to the snowy mountain; let him who slays not be slain." The fusion of three castes out of the four, leaving the Brahman paramount, and alone in integrity of race, is a proof of the severity of the strife. Among the millions of the Hindus, Buddha has not now a single worshiper. The minister of the powerful Akbar, in the 16th century, could find no one in the wide dominions of his master who could give him any explanation of the doctrines of Gôtama."—*Legends and Theories*, pp. 205, 206. It would seem, however, from the dates of the Mohammedan invasions that the time given by Major Cunningham above is too late. More probably it may be in the ninth or tenth century.

In exchange for some of the elements of material civilization which she borrowed thence, India gave back to Rome advanced ideas upon the great problems of life. The fine thought of the philosophers of Alexandria and the Platonic school generally, derived much of its stimulus and nourishment from the East, was Oriental speculation cast in Occidental mold. And sundry of the observances in the Catholic Church appear to have been derived from Buddhistic source. "The ideas found in the Inferno of Dante are many of them purely Buddhist." * Josaphat, who has been made a leading character in the Roman martyrology, is Sâkya-Muni transplanted and appropriated by Rome. The story was used to illustrate, as it well did, the trial and the conquest, amid great temptations, of a sensitive, saintly soul. Marco Polo said of Sâkya, "If he had but been a Christian, he would have been of the foremost in the sight of Heaven."

Undoubtedly Buddhism, as we have it, historically has been, and is, a gross idolatry, a dark, blighting paganism. It seems to have fallen towards that almost from the beginning. As had been the case with Brahmanism before it, on the one hand airy, vapid speculations arose, subtle dialectics, refining and sublimating, until they abolished everything,

---

* S. Beal.

annihilated all affirmative being, and left the spirit in the coldness and chill of mere negations;* and on the other hand a gross sensualism, that worshiped form and circumstance and person, and made the very Nirvâna low and carnal. Buddha, as the history tells, turned the wheel of the law, or taught publicly the word of life; the saints to-day perform their devotions by turning with windlass huge wheels inscribed with mystic formulas and the precepts of their prophet. Buddha proclaimed the not, rising beyond the limitations of person, and feeling the utter

* It would be of little profit here, even could we do it, to enter into any account of the Buddhistic speculation. It was very voluminous, and any tolerable sketch of it would take large space. There were many schools—sects and sub-sects, beginning with *Vaibhâschikas* and the *Sâutrantikas* (those who held most by the Abhidharma and by the Sûtras respectively), numbering at one time eighteen or twenty. Afterwards all are represented in the two Vehicles, the Great and the Little, which for many centuries contended together in debate upon their respective doctrines. And in these, especially the Great Vehicle, there were various divisions or schools. All the latitudes and realms of subtle, abstract thought were traversed in these speculations, and the stages of the ancient Greek philosophizing, and of the mediæval scholastic, were percurred on the Eastern soil. The mysticism of the New Platonists and the idealism of Fichte is there. Says the Lânka Vatâra, a book belonging to one school of the Great Vehicle, "What seems external exists not at all, only the soul manifests itself in different forms." Again it is said, "All worlds are but the creation of our thought." There is also in large measure the negation and nihilism of the Sophists, the Nominalists, and the skeptics of all ages. Those who are curious in such matters may find a sufficiently full account in Wasseljew's *Buddhismus*.

impossibility to define heaven or the beyond, dropped never a hint describing it in form; he forbore to utter any name of God, perhaps knew never a thought of personal immortality, and yet he was quickly himself apotheosized, paradise was built up filled with carnal elements, and his own name is invoked as that of a supreme deity in the skies, ready to help forever. Such is the story of Buddhism wherever it has gained possession of multitudes; such, with slight modifications, will we find it in Mongolia, in China. in Thibet, Ceylon and Farther India; more marked as an idolatry doubtless in the later time, than it was in the early periods.

But there were certain impressions laid upon it too deep to be effaced. It never lost its pacific, gentle character, never, at least in the early centuries, raised the hand of persecution or oppression, although it long had at its bidding the arm of civil power. It carried all its conquests by persuasion and the force of character. It suffered wrongs, sometimes great violence, at the hand of its enemies. We hear of wars, invasions of India, persecutions, in which many temples were burned and multitudes of Bhikshus were killed. And the Brahmanical power, as we have seen, at length arose and put the followers of Sâkya to the sword. But the same features of gentleness, reverent regard for life, forbearing to hurt the smallest creature that lives, distinguish the faith to this day. "No religion, not even the Christian," says Max Müller, "has exercised so powerful an influence on the diminution of crime as the old, simple doctrine of the ascetic of Kapilavstu." * King Asoka, whose edicts are preserved on monumental columns and on rocks, enjoins the practice of the most generous virtues, orders the construction of roads and hospitals, and even abolishes capital punishment.

"The king," he says, "beloved of the gods, honors every form of religious faith; but considers no gift nor honor so much as the increase of the substance of religion; whereof this is the root—to reverence one's own faith, and never to revile that of others."

"Alms and pious demonstrations are of no worth compared with the loving-kindness of religion. The festival that bears great fruit is the festival of duty."

"The king's purpose is to increase the mercy, charity, truth, kindness and piety of all mankind."

"There is no gift like the gift of virtue."

"Good is liberality; good, it is to harm no living creature; good, to abstain from slander; good is the care of one's parents, kindness to relatives, children, friends, slaves."

---

* Koeppen also speaks to the same effect—I., 480, 481.

"There is no higher duty than to work for the good of the whole world."

Dushtagâmini, a king of Ceylon, of the second century B. C., is recorded in the Singhalese annals to have established hospitals, endowed monasteries, opened roads through his dominions, furthered agriculture, etc. He constructed a stupendous dagoba, and the edict that is quoted from him in regard to it, declares that no part of that great work should be performed by unpaid labor.*

Megasthenes, who about 300 B. C., was sent by Seleucus Nicator to Palibothra, to the court of King Kandragupta, where he spent several years, speaks of a sect of philosophers he found there opposed to the Brahmans, the Sarmanai, presumably the Srâmanas, as they were called; *i. e.*, ascetics who subdue the senses. They live simply, he says, subsisting upon the alms that are given them; abstain from wine, and maintain most chaste celibacy.

The manners of the Mongolians have been softened, their characters very essentially ameliorated, since they came under the influence of this faith, as all travelers who have been among them abundantly testify. Indeed, the change has amounted well nigh to a transformation, as will appear by comparing

* See Johnson's *Oriental Religions*, pp. 739–741.

them since their conversion with what they were before. Murder and robbery, it is testified, in the region extending from the Great Wall to the Altai, are as infrequent today as in the civilized countries of Europe. These savage hordes were the scourge and the terror of Asia. Some of the tribes still retain their old worships and wild barbarism, and show by contrast what Buddhism has achieved for those of the same blood and natural qualities. Of the Thibetans, Neumann says, "The savage traits of these people, the mild, philanthropic doctrine of the prince Sâkya has done much to soften, if it has not eradicated." "All men," they hold, "are brothers," and they seek to treat all with the spirit of a true fraternity. The Chinese have a proverb that runs so; "Religions are many, all different, but reason is one; we are all brethren,"—which, though not directly traceable to Buddhism, probably came of that inspiration.

A like amelioration has been wrought upon the Birmese and Siamese. "Previous to its introduction," says Mr. Low, "these nations must have been savage in the extreme." Except in occasional instances of sudden heat and violent outbreaks of the savage passions—as in the case of war against enemies, in which it is said they give loose to the every revenge—they are pacific, gentle, tractable, exceedingly hospitable to strangers, and most carefully considerate to anticipate their every want. Private persons construct in Siam, at their own expense, foot-paths and bridges, and erect along the streets and water-courses places of shelter and lodging-quarters for the wayfarer. Daily the women fill vessels with fresh water along the road-side, for the traveler, whenever he shall wish, to quench his thirst. The same custom obtains also in Ceylon. Thefts and murders are comparatively unknown, the latter particularly. In the populous city of Bangkok, containing 400,000 people, very rarely, we are told, is a broil or quarrel seen, and so infrequently is murder committed, that sometimes for the space of an entire year there will not be a single case.

If, as in Japan and Siam, Buddhists have once arisen to put down with strong arm of power Christianity from their midst, it is to be remembered that this was done under the provocation of a first wanton attack, and attempted extermination of their own institutions and faith.

The testimony is abundant that the natural moralities are better observed, the chastities better maintained in the countries under the sway of Buddhism than elsewhere in the East. Tender care is taken of the sick, the aged, the helpless. Reverence to parents is made one of the first of duties. A sixth commandment (the five of universal obligation are given on page 86) imposed upon the laity in Thibet is, "Thou shalt cherish thy father and mother."

"To honor father and mother is better than to pay worship to the gods of heaven and earth."

"If a child should carry father and mother, one upon each shoulder, for a hundred years, he would then do less for them than they have done for him."

These passages of the law have become proverbs with the people.

Bigandet testifies that one effect of Buddhism, wherever it has gone and exerted anything like a decisive influence, is the amelioration — a very material one — of the condition of woman. This is marked in Siam, in Tartary, Birmah and Ceylon. And he ascribes it to the fact that this religion knows no distinctions of rank, except such as are founded in character.* There are works written by Buddhistic authors against caste, and these have been used by Christian missionaries in their warfare against that oppression.† Polygamy is not approved, albeit Buddhism sprang up and has

---

*Pp. 283, 284. "It was his (Buddha's) doctrine that it is the greater or less development of the moral principle that makes the essential difference in the status of men."— Hardy, *Legends*, etc., p. 15.

† Koeppen, I., p. 129. Here is a sample of the argument: "The foot of a tiger differs by very distinct characteristics from that of an elephant, of an elephant from that of a man; but no one can tell wherein the foot of a Brahman differs from that of a Sûdra."

grown among polygamists. In Ceylon and Birmah it is prohibited; monogamy is the rule here and in Siam, though less general in Thibet and Mongolia. Polyandry indeed prevails to some extent, as among the lower classes in Ceylon, and particularly in Thibet, but this—at any rate in Thibet—is much older than the introduction of Buddhism there, and is opposed and forbidden by Lamaism.*

Mrs. Leonowens, the English governess at the king's court in Siam, found the condition, as a whole, less favorable than the statements above, drawn from residents there, would indicate; nevertheless she instances some features that are not a little remarkable, and go to show something of the quality of the religion held there. In the temple service that she attended, the invocation is this: "O, Thou Eternal One, the Perfection of Time, Thou immutable Essence of [in] all Change, Thou most excellent radiance of Mercy, Thou infinite Compassion, Thou Pity, Thou Charity!" Then followed an exhortation to charity and kindliness, fervent, fine, such, she says, "as might be wisely imitated by the most orthodox of Christian priests." And that these are not wholly

* So, at least, it is said in Koeppen, I., p. 477, Note, though the statements, as given on opposite pages, in regard to prohibition or permission, are conflicting.

empty words, is evidenced by the acts of generous beneficence, done at some times, particularly on Buddha's birthday, to the suffering and the poor.

One of the most impressive scenes she ever witnessed, she tells us, was on the occasion of the death of a Buddhist priest, the High Priest of Siam. It was an exhibition of complete trust in the Supreme, a self-forgetfulness, devotion to the welfare of others to the very end. This was the invocation chanted by the assembled priests:

First Voice — "Thou Excellence or Perfection! I take refuge in Thee."

All — "Thou who art named Poot-thoo! — either God, Buddha or Mercy — I take refuge in Thee."

First Voice — "Thou Holy One! I take refuge in Thee!"

All — "I take refuge in Thee!"

"The absorbing rapture of that look, which seemed to overtake the invisible, was almost too holy to gaze upon. Riches, station, honors, kindred — he had resigned them all more than half a century since, in his love for the poor, and his longing after truth. He was going to his clear eternal calm. With a smile of perfect peace, he said, 'To your Majesty I commend the poor, and this that remains of me I give to be burned.' And that, his last gift, was indeed his all." *

* *English Governess at the Siamese Court*, pp. 189, 201, 202.

The late king of Siam maintained entire religious freedom for all his subjects, protected Christian churches against interference, and sought to purify Buddhism from superstition and exalt it to a pure catholic religion. The present king has abolished slavery thoughout his dominions, has broken, or is breaking up the mendicancy and idleness of the priests, sending them out to earn their living by some honest industry, and has initiated various important public improvements besides. The lesson of equal rights and equal liberties, we are told, he had lived and learned long ago, in childhood. Free churches of Buddhists who reject all that is miraculous, and adhere only to the moral teachings, have existed in that country nearly forty years.* And so we find freedom from a spirit of narrowness, intolerance, the conceit of exclusive claim, among the Buddhists to a remarkable, an unprecedented degree. They have seen far enough to discover that all religions are approximations, and the highest is but partial. Hence they have not infrequently sought to supplement their own from another. Said a Singhalese chief, who put his son in a Christian school, to the astonished missionary, "I have a like veneration for the doctrines of Christianity, as for those of Buddhism. I add your

---

* Sir John Bowring, quoted by Koeppen, I., 468.

religion to my own, in order to steady it, for I consider Christianity a very safe outrigger to Buddhism." Kublai-Khan, the great Tartar monarch, in the fourteenth century, Father Ruysbrock tells us, hearing all the advocates plead for their respective faiths at his court, declared that as the different fingers are given to the one hand, so are the religions. The Regent of Lhassa declared perpetually to the Catholic missionaries Huc and Gabet, as they tell us, "Your religion is like our own, the truths are the same; we differ only in the explanation. Amid all that you have seen and heard in Tartary and Thibet you must have found much to condemn; but you are to remember that the many errors and superstitions that you may have observed, have been introduced by ignorant Lamas, but are rejected by intelligent Buddhists." "He admitted between us and himself only two points where there was disagreement—the origin of the world and transmigration of souls." "Let us examine them both together," said he to them again, "with care and sincerity; if yours is the best we will accept it; how could we refuse you? If, on the other hand, ours is best, I doubt not you will be alike reasonable, and follow that."

"Popular education," says Bastian, "has reached a considerable degree of advancement in all Buddhist countries. Every town, almost every secluded village, has its monastery occupied by monks, who, either with or without pay, give instruction to children, affording to all the means of acquiring elemental knowledge; so that it is rare to find persons who can neither read nor write."

In the Chinese Fo worship, the Liturgy, there is recorded a vow of the Bodhisattva Kwan Yin — the great Compassionate Heart or Mercy — a high act of consecration to the service of humanity. "Never will I seek or receive private individual salvation — never enter final peace alone, but forever and everywhere will I live and strive for the universal redemption of every creature throughout all worlds. Until all are delivered, never will I leave the world of sin, sorrow and struggle, but will remain where I am." The worshipers are to seek to be filled and quickened with the same spirit, to pray and to toil for the salvation of all men. "I pray for all men, that they may attain perfection of wisdom, — may I quickly deliver all sentient creatures! — may all emerge from the wheel of transmigration and be saved." * In what Christian land shall we easily find a like generous vow of consecration?

---

* Beal's *Catena*, pp. 405, 406, 409. Also see address by Rev. W. H. Channing, on the *Religions of China*, as given in the annual report of the meeting of the Free Religious Association, 1870.

The following is given as a Mongolian prayer:

"O thou in whom all creatures trust, Buddha, perfected amidst countless revolutions of worlds, compassionate towards all, and their eternal salvation, bend down into this our sphere, with all thy society of perfected ones. Thou law of all creatures, brighter than the sun, in faith we humble ourselves before thee. Thou who completest all pilgrimage, who dwellest in the world of rest, before whom all is but transient, descend by thy almighty power, and bless us."

These show traces of a parentage that has never been effaced; they carry back to a home first in some broad, catholic soul.

III.

THE MAN AND THE THOUGHT.

IT seems possible, in a measure, to penetrate the myth and fiction, to read through the partial or awry representation of him, and learn what this man was, judge of his quality and relations, not to Indians or Mongolians simply, but to mankind. The data for forming such judgment are tolerably fair. It does not appear that he ever wrote anything. The Sûtras or discourses were put to record from memory, some time after his death * — some of them

* The Canon is said to have been settled in the first Council, held a few days after the death of Buddha, but this is doubtful. It is not probable that anything that we have, was put to record, or, at least, formally passed upon, earlier than the third Council, held in the time of King Asoka, and perhaps a good portion is not of so early a date as that. According to the Singhalese tradition the Canon was first written down considerably later, say nearly 100 B. C., and according to the Thibetan, only at the time of King Kanishka, about the commencement of our era. Still there are two or three small books, as we shall see, that probably are genuinely authentic utterances of the Master, bearing an internal character that gives them decided superiority over most of the others.

perhaps not even so good as that—but the features laid upon his institution, and current in the beliefs of his followers, are distinct enough to give a measurably clear and just view of the man.

He had doubtless, under one view, an ancestry. He was born of a thoughtful race, a people calm, contained, meditative, readily given to withdrawal from the outer, dwelling in solitudes, sitting rapt in most absorbing and subtle contemplation, such as the world has never seen before or since. Life, a perpetual change, a dream, an illusion; the seen the unreal, and the real, if anywhere, in the unseen; existence a road of births, no end to them, no limit to the limitations, transmigration of the soul forever, —this was a part of the prevailing faith, religion of saint and Brahman. Into such beliefs Gautama was born, and they must have made at the beginning a deep impression upon his susceptible nature, one that perhaps he never to the end outgrew. He was conceived in their atmosphere, and they entered the fibre of his nerves, his soul was charged with them. "There never was," says M. Müller, "a nation believing so firmly in another world, and so little concerned about this." *

* "The divinely wise rest, never more to wander, in Brahma. When the wise have attained *atman* (self, soul) then are they satisfied in

But though we can see something of the antecedents, and find a genealogy, we cannot from them account for him. History will not explain him. He came a Melchisedek, without father or mother, born from the bosom of the eternities. In that soul dwelt the infinite, deep sense of the everlasting, conscious of its origin and home, and intense yearning to return and rest there. He was of very thoughtful turn, in his early boyhood, as we saw, withdrawing himself from companions, that he might alone contemplate, retiring into groves and solitudes, that he might hold communion with unseen. Ecstatic hours seem to have visited him; he recalled with utmost fondness in after years the vision he had seen in the gardens of Lumbinî. The spectacles of life wrought their deep impression on him. This transience, never an instant of rest, this swift maturing and decay of the physical being, life but a corruscation,

---

knowledge, their being is complete, their desires are past away, they are at repose, attaining to the all-pervading Nature, they go themselves into the supreme All, sinking their soul therein. As rivers flowing to ocean disappear in it, lose their name and form, so merges the wise, emancipated from name and form, into the supreme eternal Spirit. Who knows the supreme Brahma, is himself Brahma; he lays aside all sorrow and sin; freed from the bonds of corporeity, he is immortal. Who knows the One, is delivered from birth into other worlds, and from death."—From the Upanishads, as given by Wuttke, *Geschichte des Heidenthums*, II., p. 399.

a flash in the air, a moment of speech, and the long eternity of silence behind it, before it; the earth the grave of all, and it in turn destined to its grave; no stability, no permanence anywhere —why, what an illusion, what a void it is! Why must it be that all flesh decays and melts away, the bloom of youth, the vigor of age but a rose-blossom, open and gone ere we can see it well? Alas, alas, what has man to do with pleasure; he is the dream of a dream, the sport of shadows. This thought of the transience, this spectacle of decay and swift vanishing away seems to have filled and haunted his mind. He could not solve the mystery of this fate; he became indifferent, renunciant, dwelling only on the death, uncaring for aught in life or the world of the seen.

It was, as we know, a mistake, but was it a strange or unnatural mistake, considering the antecedents and surroundings, considering his temperament, the venous blood so predominant, and considering, withal, the deep sobriety of his nature, that intense longing for substance and stay? There are minds absorbed in the sense, all engrossed with appearance and show, fleeting illusion. The multitudes in all ages are prevailingly such. There are, on the other hand, those, few in any age, who dissolve and annihilate the seen, resting only in unchanging and unseen.

Time with them is a shadow, earth and life but a *mirage*, an illusion; the objects the multitudes long for and eagerly grasp, are not the boon; the Nirvâna is other, is beyond.

Such a mind, and that preëminently, was Buddha. Early he bethought him of the problem set for working, early he resolved that it should be done. The deliverance should be wrought, the world of permanence, though it should come by renunciation, destruction of all worlds, should be found. He dedicated himself to that sublime task, and how he started, did and sacrificed, we somewhat know. In his childhood years, as would seem, there came to him the elemental riddle of being, the contradiction and towering mystery of existence, this fact of individuation, the dropping of the soul, spark of infinity, in the world of time. From this individuation, this limiting within the bounds of person, diremption of the world away from me — so that there is a somewhat not myself, not mine, or rather there is a higher, in which me, and not me, are not yet dissolved, absorbed, sublimated — from this comes our want and thirst, the perpetual reaching forth and struggle.

We have a little of the form in which he put it. "Here is lack, sorrow," said he, "perpetual through life; it comes of our affections; these affections from our individuation,* our limitations, from the fact that there is an outside, something not ourselves, and that we do not possess. We must close the chasm, extinguish the want, bridge the abyss, so that there shall be no without to this within, no lack of its possession, ere we can arrive at the supreme felicity." These are in substance, as we take it, his "sublime verities" on which so much disquisition has been had. They occupied, it is said, almost the entire time of the first Council, held immediately after his death, and they have certainly been the theme of much speculation since.

1. There is pain, sorrow in the world.
2. This comes of the desires, of lack and of sin.
3. This pain may cease by Nirvâna.
4. There is a way that leads thither.

This, too (the way), he puts under eight heads or parts. In substance they are the doctrine of perfect poise, of ethereal recognition and steady dwelling therein. "Right view," he says,—seeing all things as they are, nothing less, nothing more. This properly

---

* In the "Heart Sûtra" in Chinese, it is said, "The nature of man and his reason were originally one and undivided; simply by reason of covetous desire his true nature was perverted, and the six modes of migrational existence, and the four kinds of birth were introduced into the world."—Quoted by Beal, p. 281.

covers the whole ground; the other points are but more specific designations or applications. Among them are "right language," or perfect truthfulness,—veracity, abhorring all falsehood or pretense; "right ends;" "right methods"—nothing unlawful in the pursuit; "right remembrance"—reading aright and treasuring for life and strength all the past, communing with its reality; and "right meditation"—considering well, keeping the height, remaining apart from all illusion and intoxication. These truths he saw in vision under the tree at Bôdhimanda, and they enraptured his soul; he felt that he could well say that he was now alive, he saw, he was *wide awake.*

On the pedestal of most of the statues of the saint to-day is inscribed this passage: "It is Tathâgata (he who has traveled the same route as the preceding Buddhas), who has explained the cause of all effects proceeding from anterior cause; it is the great Srâmana likewise who has explained the cessation of these effects." Conjoined with this is a very sacred sentence in the eyes of all Buddhists, found by Csoma de Körös frequently repeated in the canonical books of Thibet, and recurring often in the Singhalese Sûtras, regarded as a kind of *résumé* of the whole doctrine: "To abstain from all sin, to practice constantly all virtue, and hold perfect mastery of one's self—this was the inculcation of the Awakened.

The ethical code corresponds to this spirit. There are five great commandments enjoined upon all:

1. Thou shalt not kill.
2. Thou shalt not steal.
3. Thou shalt not commit adultery.
4. Thou shalt not speak untruth.
5. Thou shalt not take any intoxicating drink.*

Additional and more special commands were laid upon those who took the vows and embraced the monastic life; commands touching diet, sleeping, dress, social intercourse, retirement to forests, ceme-

---

* "This law is broken by even letting fall upon the tongue only such a drop of intoxicating liquor as would hang at the end of a blade of Thaman grass, if it is known to be intoxicating. —*Buddhagosha's Parables*, Rogers' Translation.

Somewhat differently is the code given by Mrs. Leonowens, as held by the Buddhists in Siam. Every one of the commandments would seem to be for universal application. They are as follows: (The first five, it will be seen, are substantially identical with those above).

1. "From the meanest insect, up to man, thou shalt kill no animal whatsoever.
2. Thou shalt not steal.
3. Thou shalt not violate the wife of another, nor his concubine.
4. Thou shalt speak no word that is false.
5. Thou shalt not drink wine, nor anything that may intoxicate.
6. Thou shalt avoid all anger, hatred and bitter language.
7. Thou shalt not indulge in idle and vain talk.
8. Thou shalt not covet thy neighbor's goods.
9. Thou shalt not harbor envy, nor pride, nor revenge, nor malice, nor the desire of thy neighbor's death or misfortune.
10. Thou shalt not follow the doctrines of false gods."

—*English Governess, etc.*, pp. 185, 186.

teries, etc. They were to wear only the poorest of garments, which they must make with their own hands, having always the yellow vesture or cloak, symbol of their profession; to live solely upon alms; never to receive silver or gold; never to sleep under roofs, except in the inclement portions of the year; always to take plain food, and never eat—more than very slightly, if at all—after mid-day.

There are six virtues that are for all men, and though they may not lead absolutely to Nirvâna, they will put all on the road thither. Charity, purity, patience, courage, contemplation and knowledge. In practicing these "we quit the dark shores of existence, where is ignorance." Buddha came for self-sacrifice, by surrendering himself, to save the world. All who follow him must tread in these footprints. The charity and love must extinguish from the heart all egoism, so fill with spirit of devotion the possessor, that he surrenders himself utterly, forgetting everything personal, his own existence even, to save others. The highest sobriety and integrity in living are enjoined. All evil speaking, any grossness of language or empty, frivolous word is strictly forbidden. The saint must seek not farther to divide and embroil, but to reconcile those who are apart. Harmony is his aim, bringing people together. Words sweet, affectionate, grateful, reaching the heart; never a syllable spoken lightly or at random, all with a purpose, and to the purpose.

One of the virtues specially emphasized was humility. "I do not say to my disciples," declared Buddha to King Prasênajit, his friend, when requested to perform some miracles to confound his enemies, "Go, and before the Brahmans and householders work by aid of supernatural power miracles greater than man can do, but instructing them in the law I say, Live, O saints, hiding your good works and showing your sins." *

So one of the old legends reports that a poor man, with a single handful of flowers, heaped the alms-bowl of Buddha, which the rich, with ten thousand bushels, could not fill. And another says that upon a time when very many lamps were kindled in honor of Buddha, one only — that brought by a very poor woman — burned through the night, while the others, presented by kings, ministers, etc., were spent and went out. †

A prominent doctrine with the Buddhists has throughout been *Karma*, doctrine of retribution,

---

* Burnouf, *Introd.* p. 170.

† Koeppen, I., 131, quoting from a Chinese work, *Foe Koue Ki*, translated by Remusat, and from a Thibetan, *Le Sage et Le Fou*, translated by Foucaux.

present state and fortune retributive upon past, and future the sanction of all the present. Every act has endless result, takes hold constantly upon the forever. What we are and now experience is the fruit of what we have been, and what we shall be depends upon what we do, or refrain from doing now. The present existence of each, his condition, is the written record, the cumulative result of his past.

> "Each house displays the kind and worth
> Of the desires I loved before."

So the Buddhist draws lessons of wisdom, keeps unbroken patience and poise in all his experience; every calamity, every indignity or wrong offered him speaks of some desert, reminds him of some behavior in the past, ages back perhaps, whereby he has laid himself open to this and made it inevitable. Great sacredness invests the present, for if he is ever to attain Buddhahood, approach Nirvâna, he must live very superiorly every moment here. So liberty and fate coexist, interpenetrate; fate behind us, around us, present here, liberty before us, and fate sealing every act with its eternal sanctions.

The doctrine of transmigration is a very old one, and has doubtless deep truth in nature. The soul is traveling the road of birth, and is on the endless ascent. It has passed through many lives, it has many more in store. Modern science tells us in more prosaic dialect the same thing which ancient Greek and Oriental fancy had said, in its fine way, that the soul journeys from monad to God. Buddha had percurred the existences. In one account he is said to have gone through 550 lives; he had been bird, stag, elephant, etc., before he took on incarnation as son of Suddhodana. Others say he had been through all the existences of earth, sea and air, had traversed every condition of all the ages. On the point of becoming Buddha, the Awakened, he had seen in recollection the innumerable births and lives he had passed, covering the hundreds of thousands of *kotis* (a *koti*, 10,000,000 years). He was in consequence of this experience in condition to enter into the sympathies of all creatures, and all worlds, for whose redemption he must devote himself and labor.

His biographers remark with astonishment that a man who seems so thoroughly to renounce the world and all the relations of life, should have laid the emphasis he did on the domestic and social virtues. But indeed the account he makes of the ethical element, the strong insistence he lays upon high character, should have told any good observer as much, convinced him there indubitably was life and healthfulness in this faith. The duties of the household, the family relations, we are informed, *he put in the first rank.** Personally he showed himself ever full of respect and tenderness towards his mother, although he had never seen her. The legends represent him as taking great interest in her behalf, visiting that portion of the skies where she dwells, to instruct her in the law and to save her. In one of the Sûtras he is reported as speaking thus:

"Brahma, O saints, where is he? In the families where father and mother are perfectly honored, venerated, served. For, according to the Law, father and mother are for the child in the family, Brahma himself. The teacher, O saints—he is in the families where father and mother are perfectly honored, venerated, served. For, according to the Law, father and mother are for the child teacher himself.

"The altar of sacrifice,† the shrine of worship—it is in the families where father and mother are perfectly honored, venerated, served. Why this? Because, according to the Law, father and mother are for the child altar and shrine itself." ‡ If this be an incon-

---

* St. Hilaire, p. 91.

† Literally, "the fire of sacrifice," a fine allusion to the Brahmanical worship. The sacred fire was kindled upon the hearth, and upon it was offered the clarified butter to the god.—See Burnouf's *Introd.*, p. 21.

‡ Burnouf, pp. 133, 134.

sistency in Buddhism, it is, as Barthelemy St. Hilaire says, one that does it honor.

It is a great thing, he declares, that parents do for their children, in rearing them, giving them food, protection, acquaintance, so far as possible for them to afford, with the sights, the facts of the world about them. "Whereby can they repay this care? By doing what they may to enrich them spiritually, by establishing them in the perfectness of the faith, if they have it not; by bringing them to the perfectness of morality, if they have bad morals; of liberality, if they are the creatures of avarice; of knowledge, if they are in ignorance."

So in the rules laid down for the priests, we find the most minute directions, even in regard to diet, the manner of eating, etc. The priest is always to approach and partake of his food in a poised, considerate, thoughtful spirit, eating possessedly, never with the least eagerness or greed, "no mouthful larger than a pigeon's egg," and each to be thoroughly masticated and disposed of before another is taken. At the present time the requirement upon the priest in Ceylon is that he shall rise each morning before day, and the first duty that calls him is care of his person, cleansing his teeth, etc. The duty of neatness in all respects, both with regard to the body itself and the clothing worn, is sedulously enjoined, and well observed. Only with the clean body and the clean garments, they say, can be the clean mind. "When the lamp, the oil or the wick is not free from dirt, the light that is given is not clear; in like manner, when the mind is unclean, the truths necessary to be known cannot be discovered, and the rites of asceticism cannot be properly exercised. But when the body is clean, the mind partakes of the same purity; as the lamp, oil and wick, when free from dirt, give a clear light." *

The breadth and elevation of the man are indicated in the fact that he relied solely to the end upon the moral element, seeking no conquests but by persuasion. Related, as he was, to courts, finding favor with kings, he might, in the midst of the conflicts which came, have invoked the arm of civil power, and there was beyond doubt temptation that way. His enemies, the Brahmans, plotted against his life, and it would have been so natural to resist by force and throttle the conspiracies, but the thought seems never to have been entertained for a moment. The weapons were not carnal, but spiritual. Then and to this hour, so far as we can definitely learn, Buddhism was the exception, sole in all history. It

* Hardy's *Eastern Monachism*, p. 113, quoted from the Wisudhi Margga Sanné.

stands as the only great historic religion that has not, upon opportunity taken the sword to put down its enemies. That a faith so born and conditioned as this was, and overtaken at length by such cruel fortune in the land of its birth, should never have soiled its hands with violence, never have lifted the arm in resistance to persecution and extermination, deserves to be remembered and recorded to its everlasting honor.

Buddha's method was not negative, but affirmative. He sought the desired change not so much by direct attack, criticising and condemning, as by holding up the standard, presenting its beauty, and attempting to incite and ravish all in the ideal presence. Every one of the abuses of the time he sought to overthrow by the affirmative. He would destroy by supplanting, overrunning and choking out by the better. His way was to overcome evil with good, hatred with love; he knew no power for transformation so fine as this; nay, he took account of no other.

The records preserved to us in the legendary tales of the saints show to us a courage and fortitude such as belong only to earnest times, found with a people who inly believe and are dedicated to an idea.

Pûrna was the son of an emancipated slave woman, set free by her master, at her own earnest solicitation. He was reared in the paternal household, and distinguished himself early by his intelligence and sleepless activity. He acquired in trade great wealth, and enriched his family also. He went frequently upon long voyages for trade, and became erewhile the head of a band of merchants who carried on this foreign commerce. Upon one of these voyages he had as companions some merchants from Srâvastî, who night and morning engaged in the reading of sacred hymns, invocations "which bear to the other shore," and sacred texts—words from the lips of Buddha. He was struck by these novel utterances, and soon as he came to Srâvastî he repaired to Bhagavat, and embraced the new faith that so touched his heart. Dead now to the world, he wished to take up his abode henceforth with a fierce, savage tribe, whose ferocities would have frightened any courage less great than his. The teacher inclines to dissuade him from his purpose.

"The men of Sronâparânta are passionate, cruel, violent. When they shall give thee harsh, threatening words, when they shall be in rage against thee, what wilt thou think?"

"If the men of Sronâparânta do this," was the reply, "if they become mad and assail me, I will say, Good men, fine men, they are of Sronâparânta, who do not strike me with the hand, nor pelt with stones."

"But if they strike and pelt thee, what wilt thou think?"

"I shall think they are good and fine that they do not take my life."

"But if they deprive thee of life, what wilt thou?"

"I shall still think they are good and fine, in that they free me with so little pain from this body full of filth."

"It is well, Pûrna; thou mayest, with that perfection of patience which thou hast attained, fix thine abode in the country of the Sronâparântakas. Go, then, O Pûrna, *thyself delivered, deliver; consoled, console;* having reached the other shore, attained complete Nirvâna, conduct others thither."* The legend adds that Pûrna went to this redoubtable country, and by his noble spirit of patience and of love, he softened and subdued the savage people, teaching them the Law and the methods of deliverance.

Another legend gives us an account of Kunâla, with the beautiful eyes. He was the son of King Asoka. Queen Rishya Rakshita, ravished with the beauty of the youth, attempted, after the manner of Potiphar's wife, to seduce him. He repelled her advances with scorn and rebuke, and the queen resolved upon vengeance. Sent by his father to a

* Burnouf, *Introd.* pp. 252–254. St. Hilaire, *Bouddha*, pp. 96, 97.

distant province of the empire to subdue a revolted city, he was working with all success, bringing back the disaffected, and winning the love of all, when there came a mandate, under the king's seal, ordering that both his eyes be torn out. The queen had in consideration of some signal service done the king, in way of subduing a most troublesome and loathsome disease, obtained possession of the supreme power for a short space, and had this opportunity to gratify her malice against the prince. It was hard to find an executioner for an office so inhuman, not a Kandâla even consenting to serve. A deformed leper was at length found to undertake it. Kunâla submitted himself resignedly, for, he said, the wise teachers who had instructed him, had well taught the perishable character of all earthly things, and the eyes themselves had done him this service, that they had shown him that nothing abides.

One of the eyes was torn out, and at his request placed in his hand. The crowd shrieked with horror. Kunâla, handling the eye, exclaimed, "Wherefore seest thou no more, as thou hast been wont, vile globe of flesh? How self-deceived and pitiable they are, the insensate, who fasten to thee, saying, 'This is myself.'" The second eye was wrested out like the first, and Kunâla, who had lost the eyes of sense, had opened within him the eyes of the soul.

"The eye of flesh," he said, "has just been taken away, but I have acquired eyes more perfect, fine and pure, eyes of wisdom. Cast off by the king, I am become son of the great king of the Law, whose child I am called. Deprived of earthly sovereignty, which brings with it so many troubles and sorrows, I have gained sovereignty in the kingdom of the soul, where trouble and sorrow are taken away."

The prince, the story proceeds, wandered from place to place, led by his young wife, who chanted in the ears of those she met, his misfortunes and his consolations. He arrived at length at the palace of his father, who on learning the cause of his affliction, resolved to punish the queen with death. Kunâla interceded for her, and saved her; took upon himself alone all responsibility for his misfortune, which he said had doubtless come by reason of some fault committed in previous existence.*

Another legend runs on this wise: Vâsavadattâ was a courtesan at Mathurâ, very famous for her fascinations. Her servant, in buying her perfumes, etc., was wont to deal with a young merchant named Upagupta. "My child," said she, "it seems that this young man delights you very much, since you always purchase of him." "My master's daughter,"

* Burnouf, p. 403-413.

replied the servant, "Upagupta is very beautiful, very gifted and sweet, and he spends his life in observance of the Law." The words awakened in Vâsavadattâ a passionate desire for Upagupta, and she ere long sent out her servant to say, "I mean to come and find you; I desire to have love with you." Upagupta responded, "The time is not yet for me to see you." She thought his refusal was on account of lack of money to pay her price, and sent again and said, "I ask of you not a single *karshapana*, I only wish to be with you." Upagupta returned the same response as before.

Some time after, Vâsavadattâ assassinated one of her lovers, that she might surrender herself without obstruction from his jealousy, to a rich merchant that sought her. Her crime became known, and the king of Mathurâ ordered that, as a punishment, her hands, feet, ears and nose should be cut off, and she, mutilated thus, be abandoned in the cemetery. Upon hearing of this, Upagupta said, "When she went about covered with fine ornaments, richest jewels, it was not well that one who seeks enfranchisement and escape from the law of birth should see her. But now that, mutilated by the sword, she has come to the end of her pride and her joys, it is fitting to visit her." Vâsavadattâ saw him approaching, and covering up and concealing as much as she could her unsightly person from view, she accosts him: "Son of my master, when my body was sweet as the flower of the lotus, adorned with all wealth and splendor of attire, whatever could attract and intoxicate, I could not, alas, draw you to my side. But now you come to view a form whose sight no one can endure, abandoned of pleasure and of beauty, inspiring only aversion, begrimed with blood and filth." "My sister," he responded, "formerly I did not come to you, drawn, as I might have been, by sensuous love; but now I come that I may know and feel the true character of the pitiful objects in which people take delight." Then, the relation tells us, he comforted Vâsavadattâ, instructing her in the Law, bringing peace to the soul of the unfortunate. She died, making profession of faith in Buddha, "to have resurrection erewhile in the realm of the gods." * "For the sake of a celestial nymph," said Rathapâla, the Brahman, when remonstrated with by his wife for having left all, "have I abandoned the world."

Ananda, most beloved disciple, cousin to Buddha, weary and very thirsty one day from a long journey, approached a well, where he saw a young Matangî girl drawing, and asked her to give him to drink.

* St. Hilaire, pp. 100–102.

The maiden, fearing to pollute him by her touch, reminded him of her caste (she was of the Kandalas, the lowest, the outcast); and that it was unlawful for her to come near a saint. "I asked thee, my sister, neither of thy caste nor of thy family, but only for water," was the reply. In like spirit is the reply of a Buddhist saint in recent time who had come under the displeasure of a king in Ceylon, for having preached to the miserable and despised caste of Rhodias. "Religion," he responded, "should be the common boon of all."

Here we are tempted to introduce the legend of Kisâgotamî. It is in *Buddhagosha's Parables*, and has been admirably reproduced by Max Müller, in his lecture on Buddhist Nihilism.

Kisâgotamî bore a son. When the boy was able to walk by himself, he died. The young mother, in her love for it, bore the corpse about, from house to house, seeking some one that should heal it. She was recommended to apply to Buddha, who, she was assured, had some medicine that would help. She applied to the saint, and was told that he required as a condition a handful of mustard seed, mustard seed obtained from a house where no son, husband, parent or slave has died. She sought from house to house, still carrying the dead body of her son, but everywhere in vain. People said to her, "The living are few, but the dead are many." She began at length to think, "This is a heavy task that I am engaged in; I am not the only one whose son is dead. In all the Sâvatthi country, everywhere children are dying; parents are dying." Casting away the dead body of her child in a forest, she repaired to Buddha and reported the result of her search. Buddha said, "You thought that you alone had lost a son; the law of death is that among all living creatures, there is no permanence." When he had finished preaching the Law, Kisâgotamî was established in the reward of a noviciate.

Some time afterwards, as she was engaged in the performance of some religious duties, noticing the lights in the houses, now shining, now extinguished, she reflected with herself, "My state is like these lamps." Buddha, who was not far distant, sent now his sacred appearance to her, which said, just as if he himself were preaching, "All living beings resemble the flame of these lamps—one moment lighted, the next extinguished; those only who have arrived at Nirvâna are at rest." Kisâgotamî hearing this, we are told, "reached the stage of a saint possessed of intuitive knowledge."

The thing is so beautifully told in a little poem, lately written by Mr. Chadwick (Rev. John W.), that we append that here.

Kisâgotamî saw her first child's face;
She saw him grow in knowledge and in grace,
But it was only for a little space.

Kisâgotamî saw him lying dead;
Against her heart she pressed his curly head,
And forth into the neighbors' houses sped.

"Something to heal my darling's hurt," she cried.
"Girl, thou art mad," was all that each replied.
But one: "Thy cure with Buddha doth abide."

Still holding the dead child against her heart,
She found the prophet and made known her smart:
"Buddha, canst thou cure him with thy wondrous art?"

"A grain of mustard seed," the sage replied,
"Found where none old or young has ever died,
Will cure the pain you carry in your side."

Kisâgotamî wandered forth again,
And in the homes of many hundred men
She sought the seed where death had never been.

'Twas all in vain. Then in a lonely wood
Her child with leaves she buried as she could,
And once again in Buddha's presence stood.

"Daughter," he said, "hast found the magic seed?"
And she: "I find that every heart doth bleed,
That every house, of death hath taken heed."

Then Buddha said: "This knowledge is thy cure.
Thy sorrow, soon or late, for all is sure;
Therefore, my child, be patient and endure."

In the *Daily Manual for the Shaman*, in Chinese, we have an inculcation of observances, which shows that, originally at least, there was recognition of the grand symbolism that runs through all life, and an earnest effort to lift the spirit to communion on that exalted plane. Every act was to be made symbolic and sacramental, the eating and the drinking, the washing, putting on of garments, etc., had meaning, signified far more than the sense. Life itself must be made aspiration and a prayer, vision and a psalm.

On awaking in the morning, let the Shaman recite this Gâtha:

"On first awaking from my sleep,
I ought to pray that every breathing thing
May wake to saving wisdom, vast
As the wide and boundless universe."

On hearing the convent bell:

"Oh! may the music of this bell extend throughout the mystic world,
And, heard beyond the iron walls and gloomy glens of earth,
Produce in all a perfect rest, and quiet every care,
And guide each living soul to lose itself in Mind Supreme."

On rising out of bed:

"On putting down my foot and standing up,
Oh! let me pray that every living soul
May gain complete release of mind and self,
And so, in perfect Rest, stand up unmoved!"

"From earliest dawn till setting sun,
Each living soul might tend to self-advance,
Reflecting thus: 'My foot firm planted on the earth,
Should make me think, am I
Advancing on my road to Heaven?'"

On putting on the clothes:

"On binding on the sash, I pray
That every living soul may closely bind
Each virtuous principle around himself,
And never loosen it or let it go."

On washing the face:

"As thus I wash my face, I pray
That every living soul may gain
Religious knowledge, which admits
Of no defilement, through eternity."

On entering within the sacred precincts:

"Beholding the figure of Buddha,
I pray that every living thing,
Acquiring sight without defect,
May gaze upon the form of 'all the Buddhas.'"
[*i. e.*, enjoy "beatific vision."] *

There is a trace of childish ceremonialism here (and we should see the more if we followed this Manual out in all its details), which easily grows to superstition and a juggle, but the thought lying at the bottom is very fine, and provided the recognition could be kept sweet and fresh, untainted with formalism, free of any set observance, spontaneous, living, nothing could be more healthful and beautiful. The dangers of asceticism and cant, of other-worldliness, are about as formidable as those of absorption and degradation in this world. When

* Beal's *Catena*, pp. 240-243.

8

we have eyes fully open, we shall see all washing baptismal, nay, every contact, every experience purifying and quickening; sunlight, air, scenery, faces, conversation—sacred elements of healing and strength for the soul. Then that which is in part only shall be done away, and the sacraments of the church be superseded, fall obsolete in the larger, comprehending sacraments of life. The open eye, too, will see the incarnations, and commune in the visible, perpetually with invisible.

The Sûtras or discourses ascribed to Buddha, are of uncertain time and authorship, but nevertheless contain declarations not a little remarkable, and not unworthy to be attributed to the master. Like Jesus, he uses parables.

In the "Lotus of the good Law" he gives his view of the method which the wise teacher and great Nature herself employs to convey truth to man, and to arouse and incite him from his torpor.

An old man, father of a family, finds, as he returns home from abroad, his house on fire. The children are sleeping, totally unconscious of the danger, the sure death that is upon them. He calls to them, in vain; they see not the fire, and will not believe they are in any danger. He promises them fine toys;

above all, three different kinds of carriages, to amuse and delight. They leave the house, and once safe, he gives them not the three — not the carriages at all, — but a chariot, splendid beyond description. "Has the father told them a lie? No, doubtless, but has fulfilled more than his word. So Tathâgata, pitying the frivolity of men, who before the impending sorrows and calamities, are sporting and pursuing their pleasures, in accommodation to their weakness, promises them, in order to break the chains of their slavery, three 'vehicles of deliverance,' or, so many several objects of incitement and desire, to win them. Taken, as the children in the burning house, with the prize offered, they leave their attachment to the worlds, and Tathâgata gives them but one conveyance, the method of reaching perfect Nirvâna."

Upon the hearing of this parable, it is said, four of the disciples who were present, responded with another, in which they compared the race of man much to a prodigal, who, leaving the house of a rich and generous father, wandered over the world, and at length came back all unconsciously to the old home. He had lost the remembrance of his father, but by-and-by, after many and severe experiences, he comes to know him again, embraces, obeys him, and enters upon his lost possession.

Bhagavat gave other parables; this, for one. A

man, blind from birth, denied that there were colors, or sun, or stars, or beauty or deformity, or beholders for them. Against all persuasion he resisted the belief, until a certain skillful physician gave him sight. He was in transports of ecstasy, acknowledging his blindness and ignorance hitherto, and exclaiming that now he saw and knew all. But the wise Rishis, observing in him a blindness still, which was more harmful than the other, sought to purge him of his conceit. "There are worlds far beyond the reach of thy present organs. Sitting in the house, thou canst not see through the walls, the thoughts of thy fellows thou canst not read, thine own begetting, thy conception and birth thou canst not recall. How sayest thou, 'I know all?' Remember that clearness is obscurity, and the obscurities shall be seen clear." Ashamed for his presumption and conceit, he committed himself for instruction in the Law to the Rishis, and the eyes of his soul were opened, as those of sense had lately been by the physician.

Such are the hints richly scattered in these discourses, of the ethereal ideas, the truths of the upper kingdom.

IV.

SENTENCES OF SCRIPTURE.

AMONG so many words afloat ascribed to the saint, it is impossible to tell what are authentically his, but there is one portion of the Buddhistic Canon, a little book called the *Dhammapadam*, or *Footprints of the Law*, whose sentences are considered with great probability to be from his lips. It was found in Ceylon not many years since, written in the Pâli language * (the Pâli was the popular language of Mâgadha), and was published, with Latin translation, by Doctor Fausböll, at Copenhagen, in 1855. Portions of it were also rendered into English by D. J. Gogerly, a missionary (in the *Ceylon Friend*, 1840,),

* The Buddhist scriptures seem to have been written — the main portions of them at least — originally both in Sanscrit (which in the time of Buddha and probably one or two hundred years before him had ceased to be a spoken language) and in Pâli. The originals of the texts which are held by the Thibetans and Chinese are nearly all in the former, the originals in possession of the Singhalese, Birmese, etc., are in the latter. Consult Burnouf, *Introd.* pp. 15, 16; Koeppen, I., p. 186.

and the whole has recently appeared in English, from the accomplished pen of Prof. Max Müller.* The inculcations in that book are of the noblest; there is trace of the morbid element, of disparagement and renunciation, such as one finds in all Buddhism, but there are exalted views of duty, ethical precepts that fall not below the New Testament standard. We give here some of them as samples, only adding that those who wish to find more must refer to the little volume itself. The rendering is taken mostly from Fausböll or Max Müller, in a few instances, from Gogerly.

1. Mind is the root; actions proceed from the mind. If any one speak or act from a corrupt mind, suffering will follow, as the wheel follows the step of the ox that is drawing.

2. Mind is the root, etc. If any one speak or act with an elevated pure mind, then joy follows like an unwithdrawing shadow. .

3. "He insulted me, assailed me, beat me, despoiled me,"—cherishing these things in the spirit, ill feeling is not allayed.

4. "He insulted me, assailed me," etc.,—by refusing to harbor remembrance of this in the spirit, ill feeling is allayed.

---

† Published by Trübner & Co., with *Buddhagosha's Parables*, London, 1869, and reprinted since by Scribner & Co., in this country, with Prof. Müller's *Lectures on the Science of Religion*, New York, 1872.

5. For hatred never ceases by hatred, but by love; this is the everlasting law.

6. Persons do not reflect, we shall speedily die. If any do thus reflect, their quarrels speedily terminate.

7. Whoso lives, regarding the sensuous delights, putting no restraint upon inclination, knowing not moderation in eating, indolent and without force,—Mâra, temptation, shall easily overcome him, as the wind the slightly rooted tree.

8. Whoso lives, not regarding the sensuous delights, restraining inclination, knowing to be moderate in eating, faithful, strong,—temptation will be powerless against him, as the wind against the rocky mountain.

10. Who casts aside his appetites, who keeps armed with the virtues, well endowed with temperance and integrity—he indeed is worthy of the yellow garment.

11. Who deem the non-substantial substance, and the substantial without substance,—they shall never attain reality, being full of vain desires.

12. But those who hold substance for substance, and unsubstantial for unsubstantial, they attain the real, being filled with true desires.

13. As the rain breaks through an ill-thatched roof, so passion invades the thought destitute of reflection.

15. The evil doer mourns in this world, and he shall mourn in the next; in both worlds has he sorrow. He grieves, he is tormented, seeing the ill of his deed.

16. The virtuous man rejoices in this world, and he will rejoice in the next; in both worlds has he joy. He rejoices, he exults, seeing the purity of his deed.

19. A man slothful, saying many good things but not doing them, is like a herdsman, counting the kine of others, but owning none.

21. Watchfulness is the path of immortality, slothful-

ness the way of death. The watchful die not; the slothful are as already dead.

23. These wise people, meditative, steady, always possessed of strong powers, attain to Nirvâna, the highest felicity.

26. Foolish, senseless men follow sloth. The wise man keeps watchfulness as his highest treasure.

29. Alert among the sluggish, wide awake among the fast asleep, the wise man advances like a racer leaving behind the hack.

31. A *Bhikshu* (mendicant) who rejoices in watchfulness and fears sloth, moves about like fire, burning all his fetters small and large.

42. Whatever a hater may do to a hater, or an enemy to an enemy,—a wrongly directed mind will do us greater mischief.

43. Not a mother, not a father will do so much, nor any other relative;—a well directed mind will do us greater service.

49. As the bee collects nectar and departs without injuring the beauty or the odor of the flower, so the sage sojourns among men; he views their ways, and learns wisdom from their folly.

54, 55, 56 (condensed). The fragrance of the flower, or of sandal wood, or of a bottle of Tagara oil is sweet but delicate; easily arrested by the winds, it is carried whither they will. But the fragrance of the good far sweeter, regardless of winds, breathes over all lands, and exhales to the throne of the gods.*

58, 59. As the lily, growing from a heap of manure accidentally cast upon the highway, delights the soul with the delicacy of its fragrance, so the wise, the disciples of

* So one of the Upanishads has it: "As the fragrance of a blossoming tree spreads far, so the fragrance of a pure action."

the all-perfect Buddha, shine amongst the foolish, and are grateful to the gods.

64. If through life the foolish man sits beside the wise, he will not taste the law, as the ladle tastes not the soup.

65. If a discerning man for one moment only sits beside the wise, he will quickly taste the law, as the tongue tastes the soup.

71. An evil deed does not turn suddenly like milk; smouldering, it follows the fool, like fire covered by ashes.

80. Well-makers lead the water (wherever they like); fletchers bend the arrow; carpenters bend a log of wood; wise people fashion themselves.

81. As the solid rock is not stirred by the wind, so neither in reproach nor in praise is the wise man moved from his poise.

82. Wise people, hearing the law, become serene, like a deep, smooth, still lake.

85. Few are there among men who attain to the other shore; most only run up and down this.

89. Those whose mind is well grounded in the elements of knowledge, who have given up all attachments and rejoice without clinging to any thing, whose frailties have been conquered and who are full of light—they are free (even) in this world.

92. He who has no riches lives on authorized food, communes with the Void, the Unconditioned, with Nirvâna, —his way is difficult to understand, like that of birds in the ether.

94. He whose senses have come to repose, like a horse well subdued by the driver, who has cast aside pride and is free from all desire,—the gods even envy such an one.

97. He who is free from credulity, but knows the Uncreated, who has cut all ties, removed all temptations, renounced all desire,—he certainly is the greatest of men.

98. In a hamlet or in a forest, in the deep water or on

the dry land, wherever venerable persons dwell,—that place is delightful.

99. Forests are delightful; where the multitude finds no delight, there the passionless will find delight, for they seek not pleasures.

103. If one man conquer in battle a thousand times a thousand men, and if another conquer himself—he certainly is the greatest of victors.

104, 105. One's own self conquered is better than all other people. Not even a god, a Gandharva, (fairy), not Mâra can change for such an one (who has conquered himself and always restrains himself), victory into defeat.

114. He who lives a hundred years, not seeing the immortal place,—a life of one day is better if a man sees the immortal place.

121. Let no one make small account of evil, saying, It will not come near unto me; by the falling of drops the water-pot is filled, and the foolish man is filled with evil, taking it up little by little.

122. Let no one make small account of the good, saying, It will not benefit me; by the falling of drops the water-pot is filled, and the wise man becomes full of good, gathering it up little by little.

123. Let a man avoid evil deeds, as a merchant if he carries much wealth and has few companions, avoids a dangerous way; as a man who loves life avoids poison.

125. If a man offend a harmless, pure and innocent person, the evil falls back upon that fool, like light dust thrown against the wind.

127. Neither in air, nor in the depths of the sea, nor in the clefts of the mountains, is any place found where a man might be freed from an evil deed.

133. Do not speak harshly to any; those who are spoken to will answer thee in the same way. Angry speech is painful, blows for blows will touch thee.

135. As a cowherd with his staff gathers his cows into the stable, so do Age and Death gather the life of man, (gather all living).

151. The brilliant chariots of kings are destroyed, the body also becomes old and decays, but the virtues of the good know not age or decay; thus do the good say to the good.

159. Let a man so make himself as he teaches others to be; he who is well subdued may subdue others; one's own self it is difficult to subdue.

There is no doctrine of commercial substitution here, not a shade of our Western dream of atonement by vicarious blood. Indeed Spence Hardy, a Wesleyan missionary, many years resident in Ceylon, finds this one of the most hopeless things in the prospect regarding the conversion of the Buddhists; they know nothing of the salvation by blood; it is so foreign to their entire system of religion that there is found no place in the Oriental mind whereon to graft such a conception. "The Buddhist knows nothing of an atonement. * * * * In the wilderness to which he is driven, no cross does he see. no river of blood, no fountain of life, with the cheering words inscribed on the rock thât overhangs it, 'Whosoever will, let him come, and drink freely and live,'" says the missionary. Pitiable indeed! They have the notion, these poor pagans, that each must reap the fruit of his own doing, and that there is no possible device of escape. "He who dies is accompanied only by his merit and demerit; nothing else whatever goes with him," says Rathapâla.

165. By oneself, the evil is done, by oneself one suffers; by oneself evil is left undone, by oneself one is purified. Purity and impurity belong to oneself, no one can purify another.

276. You yourself must make an effort. The Tathâgatas are but preachers. The thoughtful who enter the way are freed from the bondage of Mâra.

175. Swans [wild fowl?] go on the path of the sun, they go through the ether by means of their miraculous power; the wise are borne out of this world, when they have overcome Mâra and his train.

193. A miraculous man, a Buddha, not easy to find, is not born everywhere. Wherever such a sage is born, that race prospers.

201. Victory breeds hatred, for the conquered is unhappy. He who has given up both victory and defeat, he, the contented, is happy.

204. Health is the greatest of gifts, contentedness the best riches, trust the best of relatives, Nirvâna the sum of delights.

219. Kinsfolk, friends and dear ones salute him who, far-traveled, returns home safe:

220. So, the good deeds done, welcome him who, going from this world, enters the other.

222. He who holds back rising anger like a rolling chariot, him I call a real driver; the rest do but hold the reins.

223. *By gentleness overcome anger; by good, evil; by liberality, greed; by openness and truth, dissembling and falsehood.*

224. Speak the truth; yield not to anger; give, when asked, of the little thou hast; by these three steps thou shalt go near the gods.

239. Let a wise man blow off the impurities of his soul, as a smith blows off the impurities of silver, one by one, little by little and from time to time.

247. The man who gives up himself to drinking intoxicating liquors,—he, even in this world, digs up his own root.

251. *There is no fire like lust, no bondage like hatred, no toil* (snare) *like perturbation, no river like desire.*

252. The faults of others are easily seen, one's own difficult to see; others' faults one lays open as much as possible, his own he hides, as a cheat hides the bad die from the gambler.

304. Good people shine from afar, like the snowy mountains; bad people are not seen, like arrows shot by night.

354. The gift of the law exceeds all gifts; the sweetness of the law exceeds all sweetness; the delight in the law exceeds all delights; the extinction of thirst overcomes all pain.

367. He who never identifies himself with his body and soul, and does not grieve over what is no more, he indeed is called a *Bhikshu* (mendicant, saint).

370. Cut off the five (senses), leave the five, rise above the five. A *Bhikshu*, who has escaped the five fetters,—he is called *Oghatinnas* (passed the flood).

372. Without knowledge there is no meditation, without meditation there is no knowledge: in whom knowledge and meditation are united, he surely is near unto Nirvâna.

377. As the Vassikâ-plant sheds its withered flowers, so, O *Bhikshus*, shed passion and hatred!

THE BRÂHMANA.*

385. He for whom there is neither this nor that shore, nor both, fearless, unshackled,—him I call indeed a *Brâhmana.*

386. He who is thoughtful, blameless, dwells alone, does his duties, is free from desires, has attained the highest end,—him I call indeed a *Brâhmana.*

392. After a man has once understood the Law as taught by the Well-awakened, let him worship it carefully, as the *Brâhmana* worships the sacrificial fire.

393. A man does not become a *Brâhmana* by his plaited hair, by his family, or by both; in whom there is truth and righteousness, he is blessed, he is a *Brâhmana.*

398. He who has cut the girdle and the strap, the rope with all that pertains to it, he who has burst the bar, and is awakened,—him I call indeed a *Brâhmana.*

399. He who, though he has committed no offense, endures reproach, bonds and stripes, strong in power of endurance, active in its exercise,—him I call indeed a *Brâhmana.*

406. He who is tolerant with the intolerant, mild with fault-finders, free from passion among the passionate,—him I call indeed a *Brâhmana.*

407. He from whom anger and hatred, pride and envy have dropt like a mustard seed from the point of an awl,—him I call indeed a *Brâhmana.*

411. He who has no interests, and when he has understood (the truth), does not say, How, how?—he who can *dive into the Immortal,*—him I call indeed a *Brâhmana.*

---

*The book is divided into sections called from their subjects, "Watchfulness," "Thought," "The Wise Man," "The Fool," "The Venerable," "The Way," "The Bhikshu," etc. The last is entitled "The Brâhmana."

412. He who is above good and evil, above the bondage of both, free from grief, from sin, from impurity,—him I call indeed a *Brâhmana*.

417. He who, after leaving all bondage to men, has risen above all bondage to the gods, who is free from every bondage,—him I call indeed a *Brâhmana*.

418. The hero who has conquered all worlds,—him I call indeed a *Brâhmana*.

423. He who knows his former abodes, who sees heaven and hell, has reached the end of births, is perfect in knowledge and a sage, whose perfections are all perfect,—him I call indeed a *Brâhmana*.

We add here the declaration ascribed to Gautama in that great hour when under the tree at Bôdhimanda, he attained, as he deemed, full vision, became Buddha, felt that now he saw, was emancipate and free. Filled with ecstasies of delight, he could not refrain from bursting into rapturous song. This is found also in the *Dhammapadam.** The free rendering we give here, measurably a paraphrase, but a true one, is from Mr. Alger, as it appeared in his interesting volume of selections from Oriental Poetry.†

"A pilgrim through eternity,
In countless births have I been born,
And toiled the Architect to see,
Who builds my soul's live house in scorn.

* Verses 153, 154.
† Boston, 1856.

O painful is the road of birth,
By which from house to house made o'er,
Each house displays the kind and worth
Of the desires I loved before.

Dread Architect! I now have seen thy face,
And seized thy precept's law;
Of all the houses which have been,
Not one again my soul shall draw.

Thy rafters crushed, thy ridge-pole too,
Thy work, O Builder, now is o'er;
My spirit feels Nirvâna true,
And I shall transmigrate no more."

One does not so much wonder at the enthusiastic praise bestowed by the Buddhists upon the utterances of their prophet, considering that we find such as these scattered in liberal measure in one at least of the books of their Canon. They say:

"The discourses of Buddha are as a divine charm to cure the poison of evil desire; a divine medicine to heal the disease of anger; a lamp in the midst of the darkness of ignorance; a fire like that which burns at the end of a kalpa to destroy the evils of repeated existence; a great rain to quench the flame of sensuality; a ship in which to sail to the opposite shore of the ocean of existence; a collyrium for taking away the eye-film of heresy; a succession of trees bearing immortal fruit, placed here and there, by which the traveler may be enabled to cross the desert of existence; a straight highway, by which to pass to the incomparable wisdom; a door of entrance to the eternal city of Nirvâna; a talismanic tree to give whatever is requested; a flavor more exquisite than any other in the three worlds;

a power by which may be appeased the sorrow of every sentient being."

In another place it is declared the *dharma* "shines upon the darkness of the world, as the rays of the sun, when this luminary has ascended the Yugandhara rocks, shine upon the lotus flowers of the lake, causing them to expand and bringing out their beauty."* "His doctrine," says the author of a legend we find in the Chinese, "he described as the centre of invariable splendor, as the incomplete and the full, *the unutterable and the ever spoken*, as something which *cannot be heard, and yet is ever heard.*" "Bright as a mirror," he adds, "was the opening of his wisdom's store, lofty as the mountains, deep as the sea, like the thunder and the lightning flash was the brilliancy and the depth of his penetration."†

The *Dhammapadam* is a very small book, a mere *brochure*, containing in all but 423 verses, but the Buddhistic Canon is very voluminous. It is divided into three parts called the *Tripitakas* or three Baskets, as the writing was originally upon palm leaves, which were placed for keeping in baskets.‡ The first contains

* Hardy, *E. M.*, pp. 192, 193, 198.

† Beal's *Catena*, pp. 136, 142.

‡ See Wasseljew, p. 118. So also now, according to him, the Thibetans and Mongolians keep their sacred books (upon paper) in baskets.

the Sûtras or discourses (to which the *Dhammapadam* belongs); the second, Vinaya, or morality, mainly a positive code for the direction of the priests; and third, the Abhidharma, or by-law, a system of metaphysics. Much of this is doubtless later, perhaps by several generations than Buddha, though all is of course ascribed directly to him, or to his immediate inspiration. In Thibet they have two gigantic collections, the *K'anjur* and the *Tanjur*, the first consisting in the different editions of 100, 102 or 108 folio volumes, and containing 1,083 distinct works, the latter of 223 folio volumes, each of which weighs in the edition of Peking from four to five pounds. These works, it is ascertained, are translations from Sanscrit originals, copies of which, in part at least, have been found in Nepal.* In China the Canon includes 1,440 distinct works, comprising 5,586 books.† The Pâli originals found in Ceylon, less voluminous indeed, are still large, containing, according to Spence Hardy, 592,000 stanzas (this, however, includes both the text and the commentaries), and have in turn been rendered into Birmese and Siamese. It is to be hoped that the substance or

---

* The Buddhist Canon in China, says Mr. Edkins, is seven hundred times larger than the Bible.

* See a good account of the character and contents of these books in Koeppen, II., pp. 278–282.

the better portions of these may be given in an English or some other European dress. There may quite likely be choice gems exhumed from this mass of speculation and dreams.

The Chinese have a little work they call "The Sûtra of Forty-two Sections." It was brought to China from India in the first century of our era,* and would seem certainly at that date to have held high place as an authority, since it was deemed the one book most fittingly representing the doctrines of the teacher, for those to whom the new word was then being carried. We select a few of them to show the quality. The translation is by Mr. Beal.

7. Buddha said: A man who foolishly does me wrong, I will return to him the protection of my ungrudging love; the more evil comes from him, the more good shall go from me; the fragrance of these good actions always redounding to me, the harm of the slanderer's words returning to him. For as sound belongs to the drum, and shadow to the substance, so in the end, misery will certainly overtake the evil doer.

8. Buddha said: A wicked man who reproaches a

---

† So says Beal, p. 189, resting apparently upon a Chinese authority. But may it not have been brought in earlier? The Buddhistic faith was introduced into China very early, and from Turkistan, where they had at the time only the doctrines of the little Vehicle (primitive Buddhism, or nearly that), and this Sûtra would seem to belong to the earliest age, and might very naturally have come through that source. See Wasseljew, p. 100.

virtuous one, is like one who looks up and spits at Heaven; the spittle soils not the Heaven, but comes back and defiles his own person. So, again, he is like one who flings dirt at another, when the wind is contrary; the dirt does but return on him that threw it. The virtuous man cannot be hurt; the misery that the other would inflict comes back on himself.

10. Buddha said: * * To feed one good man is infinitely greater in point of merit than attending to questions about heaven and earth, spirits and demons. These matters are not to be compared to the religious duty we owe to our parents. *Our parents are very divine.*

11. Buddha said: There are twenty difficult things in the world—being poor to be charitable; being rich and great, to be religious; to escape destiny; to get sight of the Scriptures; to be born when a Buddha is in the world; to repress lust and banish desire; to see an agreeable object and not seek to obtain it; to be strong without being rash; to bear insult without anger; to move in the world without setting the heart on it; to investigate a matter to the very bottom; not to contemn the ignorant; thoroughly to extirpate self-esteem; to be good, and at the same time to be learned and clever; to see the hidden principle in the profession of Religion; to attain one's end without exultation; to exhibit in a right way the doctrine of expediency; to save men by converting them; to be the same in heart and life; to avoid controversy.

13. Buddha said: Who is the good man? The religious man only is good. And what is goodness? First and foremost *it is the agreement of the will with the conscience* (Reason). Who is the great man? He who is strongest in the exercise of patience. He who patiently endures injury and maintains a blameless life—he is a man indeed!

14. Buddha said: A man who cherishes lust and desire,

and does not aim after (see) supreme knowledge, is like a vase of dirty water, in which all sorts of beautiful objects are placed — the water being shaken up men can see nothing of the objects therein placed; so it is, lust and desire, causing confusion and disorder in the heart, are like the mud in the water; they prevent our seeing the beauty of supreme reason. But remove the pollution, and immediately of itself comes forth the substantial form. So also when a fire is placed under a pot, and the water within is made to boil, then whoever looks down upon it will see no shadow of himself. So the three poisons which rage within the heart, and the five obscurities which embrace it, effectually prevent one attaining (seeing) supreme reason. But once get rid of the pollution of the wicked heart, and then we perceive the spiritual portion of ourselves which we have had from the first, although involved in the net of life and death — gladly then we mount to the Paradise of all the Buddhas, where reason and virtue continually abide.

15. Buddha said: A man who devotes himself to Religion is like one who takes a lighted torch into a dark house; the darkness is at once dissipated, and there is light! Once persevere in the search after wisdom, and obtain knowledge of truth — error and delusion entirely rooted out — oh! what perfect illumination will there be!

16. Buddha said: In reflection, in life, in conversation, in study, I never for a moment forget the supreme end, Religion (Reason).

18. Buddha said: Throughout an entire day's conduct to keep the thoughts steadily on Religion (Reason), and from this religious conduct to realize a deep principle of Faith — this indeed is blessedness without measure.

21. Buddha said: A man who rudely grasps after wealth or pleasure, is like a little child coveting honey cut with a knife; scarcely has he had one taste of its

sweetness, before he perceives the pain of his wounded tongue.

24. Buddha said: Lust and desire, in respect of a man, are like a person who takes a lighted torch and runs with it against the wind. Foolish man! not letting go the torch, you must needs have the pain of a burnt hand; and so with respect to the poison of covetousness, lust, anger, envy; * * the misery to the person will be just like the self-inflicted pain on the hand of the foolish man bearing the torch.

28. Buddha addressed all the Shamans—Guard against looking on a woman. * * If you must needs speak to her, let it be with pure heart and upright conduct. Say to yourself—"I am a Shaman, placed in this sinful world; let me be then as the spotless lily, unsoiled by the mud in which it grows." Is she old? Regard her as your mother. Is she honorable? Regard her as your sister. Is she of small account? Regard her as a younger sister. Is she a child? Treat her reverently and with politeness.

34. Buddha said: The practice of Religion is just like the process followed in an iron foundry. The metal, being melted, is gradually separated from the dross and drops down; so that the vessel made from the metal must needs be good. The way of wisdom is likewise a gradual process, consisting in the separation of all heart pollution, and so by perseverance reason is accomplished.

40. Buddha said: A man in the practice of Religion, who is able to destroy the root of lust and desire in himself, may be compared to a person who counts over his beads. One by one he counts them, till the whole be finished. So when there is an end of wickedness, reason is attained.

42. Buddha said: I regard the dignities of kings and princes as the dust-motes in a sunbeam; the value of gold and jewels as that of a broken platter; dresses of the finest silk I regard as the scraps of silk given as presents. I

regard the collective chiliocosm as the letter "A" (the symbol of the earth). The different expedients in religious practice I regard as a mere raft to carry over the treasure. * * I regard the state of perfect mental equilibrium as the true standing ground, and all the various forms of apparitional existence as the changes of vegetation during the four seasons.*

"It (the Law) is as a cloud which with a garland of lightning spreads joy on the earth; the water falls on all creatures, herbs, bushes, trees, and each pumps up to its own leaf and blossom what it requires for its several end. So falls the rain of the Law upon the many-hearted world. The Law is for millions; but it is one and alike beautiful to all; it is deliverance and repose."*

And the Singhalese ascribe this to Buddha:

"Out of mud springs the lotus flower; out of clay come gold and many precious things; out of oysters the pearls; the brightest silks to robe fairest forms are spun by a worm; bezoar from the bull, musk from the deer are produced; from a stick is born flame; from the jungle comes sweetest honey. As from sources of little worth come the precious things of earth, so is it with hearts that hold their fortune within. They need not lofty birth nor noble kin. Their victory is recorded."

One of the school reading-books, we are told, put into the hands of the juveniles in Ceylon, is a collection of maxims in Sanscrit by a Rishi, Wâsana. It contains sentences which, if not regarded as

---

* Beal's *Catena*, pp. 193, 199, 201, 203.

* From the *White Lotus of the Good Law.*

canonical, well deserve careful recording and remembrance:

"As drops of water falling into a vessel gradually fill it, so are all science and instruction and riches to be acquired."

"Though the good have only a little wealth, like the water of a well, it is useful to all. Though the bad have much wealth, like the salt water of the sea, it is useful to none."

"The evil man is to be avoided, though he be arrayed in the robe of all the sciences, as we flee from the serpent, though it be adorned with the kantha jewel."

"We must be deaf in hearing the evil of others, blind in seeing the imperfection of others; as those without members in committing sin, and as those without a mind in thinking to do wrong."

"The pearls and gems which a man has collected, even from his youth, will not accompany him a single step towards the future world; friends and relatives cannot proceed a step further than the place of sepulture; but a man's actions, whether they be good or bad, will not leave him, they will follow him to futurity."

"A good action done in this world will receive its reward in the next; even as the water poured at the root of a tree will be seen aloft in the fruit and the branches."*

The following are among the common maxims of the priests of Siam:

"Glory not in thyself, but rather in thy neighbor."
"Cause no tree to die."
"Eat nothing between meals."

---

* Hardy's *Eastern Monachism*. pp. 316, 317.

"Use no perfume but sweetness of thoughts."

"Be lowly in thy thought, that thou mayest be lowly in thy act."

"Do no work but the work of charity and truth."

"Contract no friendship with the hope of gain."

"Borrow nothing, but rather deny thy want."

"Lend not unto usury."

"Keep neither lance nor sword nor any deadly weapon."

"Judge not thy neighbor."

"Be not familiar, nor contemptuous."

"Labor not for hire, but for charity."

"Look not upon women unchastely."

"Give no medicines which contain poison, but study to acquire the true art of healing, which is the highest of all arts, and pertains to the wise and benevolent."

"*Love all men equally.*"

"Perform not thy meditations in public places."

"Make no idols of any kind."*

---

* Mrs. Leonowens' *English Governess, etc.*, p. 203.

V.

THE DOCTRINE.

IT is plain that this man, Buddha, is an observer, he has seen things, read secrets, he is of poetic temperament, he discerns the relations, the harmonies of the world, and uses well the language of symbol. May we not add also that the indications are of an experience, that he has lived, and incarnated the ideals in history?

Probably there has never been a system of morality so purely unselfish offered to the world. It held out no rewards, recognized not even the personal existence of the saint as a thing to be preserved at all; it was pure renunciation, divorce from all regard for one's self. The individual may perish, humanity, the great interests of truth and virtue, welfare of the universe, shall live. I am to die and be extinguished for the life of the world. We compare this man here with the saint we all venerate, the Jesus all our Western world prays to, and the comparison is not unfavorable to the former.

Jesus seems to have been not quite uniform, forgetting himself and preaching now the doctrines of noblest self-renunciation, then again somewhat asserting himself and making great promises in this life and the life to come to his chosen ones. Sâkya-Muni does this last, never. He offers throughout no rewards other than self-denial and virtue itself. The self, the person is so far forgotten that he seems extinguished in the work and the grand destiny. Man is to be glorified in humanity. And so the doctrine has been thought but a gospel, if such a word may come in, of annihilation. There are no conquests, no power, no wealth in store. In this we think Sâkya-Muni is not the inferior of the Galilean youth. It is said that this is taking us to an atmosphere of great rarity, that few here can respire. It may be true, but it indicates the elevation of the founder of this faith, that he would know nothing at all save the great verities that are the life and the end of man, and before which all else is as naught.

Of course it is difficult to see how we are to part with our own existence, or how lose sight utterly of ourselves. The denial is subsumed by affirmation, and renunciation is constantly transmuting in our thought to possession. The nice metaphysics no acuteness can fathom. Buddha doubtless saw also this fact of the real, and such terms as "the other life," "the highest blessedness," etc., as the synonyms of Nirvâna, indicate well that he made true recognition. But he was certainly right in insisting upon the not, and guarding well against all worship of the determinate and known, and so against the subtle lapse into idolatry. Had men always been thus careful against absorption, there had never been any idolatry.

Buddhism, it has been said, has no God, and the charge of Atheism has been laid against it widely, and on the part of many who ought to know whereof they affirm. Doubtless in the ordinary or current theological sense of the word, Buddha was an Atheist. He never refers, so far as we know, to any supreme personal Being, to any individual God. "There is a supreme power, but not a supreme Being," says Spence Hardy, characterizing the doctrines now current under the name of Buddha. In reference to human existence, he does not seem to regard personality of the individual as permanent, but rather as something phenomenal and transient, the result itself perhaps of some lapse or disorder, and in the enlarging destiny of the soul to pass away.* At any rate, whatever he

* In an edition, or rather abstract, of the *Prajna Pâramitâ* (Absolute Wisdom), a work belonging to the great Vehicle school (in the

may have thought of personality *per se*, he forbore steadily from making any impersonation of God. He knows no person but the sublime verities into which all things melt and sublimate, and which again are chiefly significant in their practical relation to us, and named by him Truth or the Law. Here he is a believer, a deep, an emphatic believer. Sterner stress one could not lay than did he upon their great reality and all commanding worth for man. He seems to have been conscious of the impenetrable mystery that hides the One from the ken of all vision, even conceptual; aware too of the swift danger there is of idolatry, in framing any impersonation, and so he holds himself to the recognition of the transcendent verities, the things that may be well called in the language of some of the old thinkers *τὰ νοητά*, "the intelligibles." What he would have said if undertaking to define his view upon the unseen, it is quite impossible for any one now to know. He seems to have fancied little the extended abstract speculations, was disinclined to spend time upon subtleties that elude all human grasp. "The ideas of being and not being," he says, "do

---

scholastic period), we have this declaration as one of the comments of Theen Tai. "The spiritual body, as to its substance, is like the vast expanse of Space. The nature of man and his reason were originally one and undivided." See p. 84, Note.

not admit of discussion," and probably he abstained from all attempts at speculative refining and determining, out of regard to the fact that, as he saw, the problems of the infinite were so absolutely transcendent and insolvable. In like spirit, when inquired of with reference to the world, whether it was eternal or not, he refused, it is said, to make any answer, deeming the question aimless and idle. Before the majestic presence he bowed, in view of the supreme ineffable, his spirit worshiped and celebrated, but forbore to describe its experience or to name its object.

Considering how inaccessible the fact, in what light unapproachable it dwells, how fruitless withal has been all the laborious speculation to seek and solve the infinite, and considering also what anthropomorphism there has always been, framing the unseen in sensuous image, what degradation and idolatry, and that, too, so habitually in the purest and best forms of worship, shall we not say, perhaps this man saw farther and did wiser than others? "He, the One," says Hermes Trismegistus, "with many names, and no name." Practically, God comes to us in the sublime verities, those truths and facts that are all-sovereign and eternal. True, the mind holds by inner necessity to a central unity, goes constantly from many or plural to one, a certain person in which all the impersonal matures and is crowned. And yet it is impossible to rest in person; the thought posits reality greater than person, and soars away beyond the realm of personal, and impersonal also, as *we* know the impersonal. We are impatient of limitations, and in dealing with the high spiritual reality, the absolute, must deny them. We must rest and soar, soar and rest, the rest being ever but for an instant, surrendered for new flight, lest by tarrying we be overcome on the plain. The worship must be fluid, in movement like the sea, whose waters keep their rest in flow, and are maintained sweet thereby; or as the centre of gravity is supported in one walking, by perpetually advancing step. Such is the destiny of the human soul, the stern fate appointed, transcending yet incarnating, incarnating and transcending, working new etherealizations, approaching ever, but never reaching the infinite goal. To keep the mind free, ascending, nearing more and more to essence and substance, that without form, enduring, is the prime necessity. We can lose nothing by carrying the negations to any extent, provided we include and cover all in broader affirmation. Giving up the idea of personal God, we are more than made good in the possession of a higher than person.

In the Buddhistic faith, as we have it historically,

Karma seems to have been supreme deity, "The supreme power," says Hardy, "is Karma," the law of sanctions. This destiny or fate is the providence that presides everywhere. There shall be no interposition, no help, no partialities of friendship shown you, you shall reap as you sow. Naked to the other world you shall go, carrying only your desert, your acquired character with you. The Siamese minister says, "There is no God, who judges of these acts, etc., and awards recompense and punishment, but reward or punishment is simply the inevitable effect of Kam (Karma), which works out its own results." In other words, as we should say, the supreme is incarnated, enthroned in the sovereign laws; these are omniscient and self-executive. This is not a harmful atheism.

Curiously enough, it seems to this heathen that the religions of the world divide here. "There are philosophers who say that all known sects may be classed under two religions only—the Brahmanyang and the Samanyang. All those who pray for assistance to Brahma, Indra, God the Creator, angels, devils, parents, or other intercessors or possible benefactors, all who believe in the existence of any being who can help them, and in the efficacy of prayer, are Brahmanyang; while all who believe they must depend solely on the inevitable results of their own acts, that good and evil are consequences of preceding causes, and that merit and demerit are the regulators of existence, and who therefore do not pray to any to help them, and all those who profess to know nothing of what will happen after death, and all those who disbelieve in a future existence, are Samanyang." *

Much, very much inquiry, has been expended upon the Nirvâna of Buddha, its proper purport and meaning in the mind of the saint. The opinion is largely held that the doctrine is nihilistic, that the goal it proposed to all the life-long endeavor was the gulf of annihilation. So it has been considered to be dark and cheerless to the last degree, fit only for madmen. Doubtless, in their works of metaphysics, the Buddhists have furnished some ground for the suspicions and charges entered against them. And what school of subtle and over-refining philosophy has not? The Greek dialecticians and the middle-age school-men did this, and in India we have, as Cousin long ago well remarked, "an epitome of the entire history of philosophy." All the phases of Western thought have been repeated, and with an added emphasis and intensity in the Eastern mind.

But in the case of Buddha himself, and quite

Modern Buddhist, p. 37.

probably that of his near followers, the criticism is, we think, at fault. It has not apprehended him. He seems nihilistic because he is so purely spiritualistic. He has to deny and keep on repeating denial, to pave the way for the only possible affirmation. He can suffer no representation of the Infinite Good for the soul. It is so good, it cannot be described, or even thought. The law is so high that it cannot be cast in form, it flies and soars away from every determination. Eye hath not seen nor ear heard. Nirvâna is the ineffable, the untold and unknown. It is the light that is darkness to our eyes. It is the *not* and the *is*; *is* qualified by *not*, and *not* transcended and extinguished by *is*. Buddha was conscious of the impotence of speech to name, or thought to apprehend, and he made no attempt to define except on the side of negation. But that he held it in the affirmative, we may not doubt.

Plainly we must in fairness interpret the Nirvâna for him in consistency with his high practical character. No man who laid such emphasis on the royal virtues, who was himself so devoted, with a lover's enthusiasm, to humanity, who had a heart so tender and warm, could be absorbed and lost in nihilism. This belongs to renunciants, to withdrawn dreamy speculators, and not to great doers. His devotion, self-sacrifice, quenchless benevolence and love, place him the peer of the highest saints of history.

"Watchfulness," he declares, "is the path of immortality, slothfulness the way of death; the slothful are as if already dead."

"These wise people, meditative, persistent, always possessed of strong powers, attain to Nirvâna, the highest felicity."

"—Nirvâna—the sum of delights."

"Who is filled with desire for the Ineffable (Nirvâna), who is rich within, whose thoughts are not hampered by any thirst,—him I call *Udhamsolas* (borne aloft)."

"Who can dive into the Immortal—him I call a *Brâhmana*."

"O *Bhikshu* (saint), empty this boat! emptied it will go quickly; having cut off passion and hatred, thou wilt go to Nirvâna."

"The sages who injure no one, who always control their body—they will go to the immortal abode, where, if they have gone, they will never sorrow more."

"When you have understood the destruction of all that was made, then you will understand that which was not made (Nirvâna)."

"The man who is free from credulity, but knows the Uncreated (Nirvâna), who has cut all ties and taken away all temptation, renounced all desires—he is the greatest of men." *

In the Chinese we have a Sûtra which has a passage on this wise:

"Basita said, Gautama, there are four kinds of condition in the world which are spoken of as non-existent; the first that which is not as yet in being, like the pitcher to be made out of the clay; secondly, that which having existed, has been destroyed, as a broken pitcher; third, that which consists in the absence of something different from itself, as we say the ox is not a horse; and lastly that which is purely imaginary, as the hair of the tortoise, or the horn of the hare. If then, by having got rid of sorrow, we have arrived at Nirvâna, Nirvâna is the same as nothingness, and may be considered as non-existent; but if so, *how can you define it as permanence, joy, personality and purity?*

"Buddha said, Nirvâna is of this sort: it is not like the pitcher not yet made out of the clay, nor is it like the nothingness of the pitcher which has been broken; nor is it like the horn of the hare, nor the hair of the tortoise, something purely imaginary. But it may be compared to the nothingness defined as the absence of something different from itself. As you say, although the ox has no quality of the horse in it, you cannot say that the ox does not exist; and though the horse has no quality of the ox in it, you cannot say that the horse does not exist. Nirvâna is just so. In the midst of sorrow there is no Nirvâna, and in Nirvâna there is no sorrow. So we may justly define Nirvâna as that sort of non-existence which *consists in the absence of something essentially different from itself.*"

* *Dhammapadam*, 21, 23, 204, 218, 411, 369, 225, 383, 97.

Terms in Chinese for defining Nirvâna, which may be rendered "passive splendor," and "brightness and rest," are constantly in use in the later scholastic works on Buddhism. The aim is to denote the perfect union of activity and repose, of motion and rest, as the sun or the moon, they say, constantly emits or reflects rays of light, and yet is ever substantially at rest.* In Birmah, Nigban (Nirvâna) is defined simply as freedom from old age, disease and death.

"All along," says Mr. Beal, "Buddhism assumes that the same condition awaits the emancipated soul as is enjoyed by the Supreme Mind."

"In Nirvâna" [with the Northern Buddhists] says Bastian, "is no longer either birth or death; only the essence of life remains. Nirvâna is nowhere (in no special place), only because it is all-embracing and all-pervading." "Far from being annihilation, as such, it is in fact annihilation of delusion, and therefore the real itself." "Lovely is the glorious realm of Nirvâna," say the Siamese, "the jeweled realm of happiness."

In this connection comes naturally the doctrine of Dhyâna, of which so much is made in this faith. It seems essentially one with the ecstasy of the old

---

* Beal's *Catena*, p. 250.

mystics. It hints the withdrawal, the emancipation of the soul from all shackles, outer or inner, till it arrives at the perfect liberty, perfect possession and deliverance into the infinite repose. The saint must withdraw into complete solitude, abdicating all care and unrest. He knows only one desire, desire for Nirvâna. Satisfaction succeeds, he enjoys this presence and is content. But satisfaction itself must cease, and all ratiocinative or thinking process; enjoyment must come in so high that it knows not joy. Self-consciousness, feeling, must pass away; pleasure as pain, memory and all knowledge fade and be known no more. And now, in the fourth stage, as it is called, the doors of Nirvâna open. The consciousness has transcended the consciousness of self, the knowledge all determinate knowing; there is no desire, no lack, no action; there is exaltation and absolute repose. The Buddha, one awakened and enlightened, now passes into infinity, infinity of space, of intelligence, into region of naught, *i. e.*, not aught. Nay, the naught itself must be annihilated, and is transcended by a larger generalization, an absolute which is neither naught nor not naught, a sphere wherein is neither idea of being nor non-being, nor non-idea of either. Such a giddy flight, such a culmination of the abstract, was hardly possible with any other than an Oriental mind. It was ecstasy and absorption, but not absorption into substance or God, since Buddha recognized in no determinate idea either substance or the divine.

Buddha is said to have passed through the four stages of Dhyâna once, and to have been making the passage into the fourth, as under the Sâl tree he entered Nirvâna.

The recognition of the transcendent character of the spiritual, the subtle and the impalpable essence of the unseen, and the struggle of the soul with the embarrassments of form and sense, the willingness, but inability, to rise beyond the time and space conditions, which with their hard necessities are ever upon us, are well illustrated in a conversation between King Milinda and Nâgasena, a missionary, and bearing date, as would seem, a little before the beginning of our Christian era.*

The king says:

> You speak of Nirvâna; but can you show it to me, or explain it to me by color, whether it be blue, yellow, red or any other color; or by sign, locality, length, manner, metaphor, cause or order; in any of these ways, or by any of these means, can you declare it to me?
>
> *Nâgasena*—I cannot declare it by any of these attributes or qualities.
>
> *Milinda*—This I cannot believe.

---

* *Milinda Prasna*, a work in Pâli, found also in Singhalese translation. See *Eastern Monachism*, p. 7.

Nâgasena—There is the great ocean. Were any one to ask you how many measures of water there are in it, or how many living creatures it contains, what would you say?

Milinda—I should tell him that it was not a proper question to ask, as it is one that no one can answer.

Nâgasena—In the same way no one can tell the size or shape or color or other attributes of Nirvâna, though it has its own proper and essential character. A Rishi might answer the question to which I have referred, but he could not declare the attributes of Nirvâna, neither could any deva of the arupa worlds.

Milinda—It may be true that Nirvâna is happiness, and that its outward attributes cannot be described; but cannot its excellence or advantages be set forth by some mode of comparison?

Nâgasena—It is like the lotus as it is free from klêsha (the lower desire), as the lotus is separate from the mud out of which it springs. It is like water, as it quenches the fire of klêsha, as water cools the body; it also overcomes the thirst for that which is evil, as water overcomes the natural thirst. It is like a medicine, as it assists those who are suffering from the poison of klêsha, as medicine assists those who are suffering from sickness; it also destroys the sorrow of renewed existence, as medicine destroys disease; and it is immortal, as medicine wards off death. It is like the sea, it is free from the impurity of klêsha, as the sea is free from every kind of defilement; it is vast, infinite, so that countless beings do not fill it, as the sea is unfathomable and is not filled by all the waters of all the rivers. It is like space, as it is not produced (by any exterior cause); it does not die, does not pass away, is not reproduced; it has no locality; it is the abode of the Rahats and Buddhas, as space is the habitation of birds; it cannot be hid, and its extent is boundless. It is like the magical jewel, as it gives whatever is desired.

It is like red sandal wood, as it is difficult to be procured; its perfume is also peerless, and it is admired by the wise. It is like Mahâ Mêru, as it is higher than the three worlds, its summit is difficult to be attained; and as seeds will not vegetate on the surface of the rock, neither can klêsha flourish in Nirvâna; and it is free from enmity or wrath.

Again he says:

It cannot be said that it is produced nor that it is not produced; that it is past, future, or present, nor can it be said that it is the seeing of the eye or the hearing of the ear, or the smelling of the nose, or the tasting of the tongue, or the feeling of the body.

Milinda—Then you speak of a thing that is not; you merely say that Nirvâna is Nirvâna; therefore there is no Nirvâna.

Nâgasena—Great king, Nirvâna *is;* it is a perception of the mind; the pure delightful Nirvâna, free from ignorance and evil desire, is perceived by the Rahats who enjoy the fruition of the paths.

Milinda—If there be any comparison by which the nature or properties of Nirvâna can be rendered apparent, be pleased thus to explain them.

Nâgasena—There is the wind; but can its color be told? Can it be said that it is in such a place, or that it is small or great, or long or short?

Milinda—We cannot say that the wind is thus; it cannot be taken into the hand and squeezed. Yet the wind *is*. We know it because it pervades the heart, strikes the body, and bends the trees of the forest; but we cannot explain its nature or tell what it is.

Nâgasena—Even so Nirvâna *is; destroying the infinite sorrow of the world,* and presenting itself as the chief happiness of the world, but its attributes or properties cannot be declared.

There is close similarity here in the illustration employed from the wind, and that of Jesus, in describing the being born of the spirit.

Again Nâgasena, in response to the king, who, unable to get out of the space conditions, continually plies the question "Where is that place?" declared it is

Neither in the east, south, west or north, neither in the sky above nor in the earth below, nor in any of the infinite sakwalas is there such a place, but wherever the precepts can be observed. And there may be observance in Yawana, China, Milâta, Alanda, Kôsala, the summit of Mahâ Mêru, or the brahma-lôkas; it may be anywhere, just as he who has two eyes can see the sky from any or all of these places, or as any of these places may have an eastern side.

Milinda asks:

Does the All-wise (Buddha) exist?

Nâgasena—He who is the most meritorious (Bhagavat) does exist.

Milinda—Then can you point out to me the place in which he exists?

Nâgasena—Our Bhagavat has attained Nirvâna, where there is no repetition of birth; we cannot say that he is here or that he is there. He is like the sun that has set behind the Astagiri mountain; it cannot be said that he is here or that he is there, but we can point him out by the discourses he delivered; in these he still lives.*

---

* *Eastern Monachism*, pp. 297. 298, 295, 299, 300.

Nirvâna is the house not made with hands, the abode beyond all abodes, the world we aspire to, transcending all, taking constantly form in our thought, but not to be cast in form, the ethereal reality soaring on and on beyond every thing determinate forever. It is gained through renunciation, through surrender and the higher choice continually. It is found in pursuit and rest, activity that is repose and perpetual possession. Giordano Bruno hints it when he sings,

—— "*nascendo il pensier, more il desio.*"
– At the birth of thought desire dies away.

It is the dream of life, the ideal felicity, that all more or less clearly discern, or at least feel and pant for, but fewest, even in remote approximation, attain. It is the infinitude of God, the heritage and longing and goal ever of the finite soul. It is that everlasting trust that rests and believes when all fails, assured that there can be no failure, that all things work together for good. It is the dwelling in "the adequate ideas," as Spinoza terms them, those supreme considerations that lift beyond temptation and all allurement. It is perpetual flowing and ascending, no pause, no attachment or fastening anywhere, and yet the deepest, a constantly increasing hold upon substance, and the abiding. In a word, it is realization and aspiration, satisfaction and thirst in one.

The complete attainment by any one would be the fulfillment of all dreams, the accomplishment of every prophecy, the subjection—aye, the elimination of time from the soul. It is the goal, boundless, everlasting, infinitely removed, yet most intimately present, which we are each ever to near, but never to reach. Buddha saw it and sang it, and fain would he rend the barrier and enter into full possession. The great reconciler, the redeemer, has not yet come, the desire of all nations is awaited still. All hitherto have been but forerunners of the Messias, Baptists in the wilderness, shouting, "Prepare, prepare ye the way." Ages, and perhaps millenniums, must yet pass ere the great synthesis shall be wrought and the mystery of being be dissolved and absorbed in spirit. We look for him that should come, and we recall that there shall be no person, that the secret is too deep and subtle that any human tongue can ever tell. But looking back over history, we find some indications that this Indian saint had partially clear vision, that he sighted, albeit dimly and from afar, the infinite goal.

Buddha did not perhaps draw the affirmations as he ought, dwelt too much in negation. The thought affirms, builds, and amid every denial constructs new positive. This is all safe while it continues transcendent and on-flowing. But the entanglements are so numerous and ever recurring, the fatality in all history has been shown so constantly in pausing and making the form the *eidolon*, that we may deem his jealousy of any worship of the determinate as rather a merit than a defect. Under this wholesome restraint it was, doubtless, that he forbore to describe God as a person, for he would admit nothing unworthy, would not profane the idea within him of the illimitable.*

The great fact of this transiency and decay in existence staggered him, it fairly haunted his brain, and he sought by all means possible to find some solution. Why must it be that life is such a flitting shadow on this earth, that it is but the lightning gleam in the sky, but the scintillation of a spark? Upon that he toiled and wrestled. Could he rend that mystery and see the eternal bloom, the youth

---

* Buddha said: "As the great universe has no boundary, and the eight quarters of Heaven no gateway, so Supreme Reason has no limits; to measure boundless space would be difficult indeed."

Confucius said: "Look up at it; it is higher than you can see! Bore into it; it is deeper than you can penetrate! Look at it as it stands before you; suddenly it is behind you;" *i. e.*, it cannot be grasped.

Lau-tsze said: "Looking up, you cannot see the summit of its head; go behind it, you cannot see its back."

that never dies, the perennial, time no more—this were the privilege, the boon of all others. The problem remains to us all unsolved. Old age comes to us as fate; no one accepts death from choice. Who does not witness with pain and a measure of sorrow the furrows come and deepen, the sure marks of advancing age and decay? Will any explain the high necessity for all this transiency and inevitable death? Broadly considered, however, the problem will probably be found a part of the question of time, the mystery of history, of birth and movement, to be be solved only when we are able to read the enigma of being. Since the river flows why must there not be emptying into the sea? We may well see to it that there be no hastening on sensuous or trivial grounds, and withal that we ourselves acquiesce, descend into the stream and make the inevitable wear connect with work, answer some solid, worthy purpose. We have seen Buddha's suggestion as to the method of disarming the king of his terrors, of working conquest over death. Brief hint as it is, it has meaning, and intimates the proximate solution. By following this road we certainly approach the true Nirvâna.

"To crowd the narrow span of life
With wise designs and virtuous deeds;
So shall we wake from death's dark night,
To share the glory that succeeds."

The very defects of Buddhism—and we see it to have had a morbid, chilling element—come in a sense from its greatness. It was so penetrated with thought of the spiritual, that it discerned nothing of the seen or material, saw eternity so large and sole, that there was no place for time. Life shrinks to nothing, for the immense beyond overshadows, annihilates it. And so the faith was renunciant, solitary, mournful. It dwelt on the dark and ghastly, lacked the element of appreciation and cheer. How it disparaged all things of time! The saints were to dwell on death, dress in rags, spend nights in cemeteries, meditate on the inevitable destruction to all. Earth is made a wilderness, a charnel-house, a dismal, mouldy tomb. Such disparagements of life and its scenes, of the human body and its enjoyments, one could never wish a second time to see, as they are in these scriptures. It is grim and ghastly. We say instinctively, a mistake, a blighting, fatal error. It was a plunge of the Oriental thought in the dim regions of Pluto and nothingness. With our Western temperament and habits we cannot abide it. But for the Eastern soil it was hardly strange, or perhaps we may say, absurd.

Nor is it in this character quite singular or certainly sole in history. We need not go far from home to find the like of it. In our current religion what depreciation and disparagement there has been, and still is, of life; such sadness, gloom, denial of all truth and beauty here.

"This life's a dream, an empty show."

"Life is but a winter's day,
A journey to the tomb."

"The brightest things below the sky
Shine with deceitful light,
We should suspect some danger nigh
Where we possess delight."

"Our life, how poor a trifle 'tis,
That scarce deserves the name."

——"The cold dreary tomb,
Sad lot of all living, mortality's doom."

Such gloomy tone runs largely in the popular hymnology. We celebrate death.

"Who, who would live alway, away from his God"—

"Ye wheels of nature, speed your course,
Ye mortal powers decay,
Fast as ye bring the night of death,
Ye bring eternal day."

"Oh, 'tis a glorious boon to die,
This favor can't be prized too high."

There are utterances in the Old Testament hardly less mournful and dreary than any that are found in the Buddhistic Canon.

"Man that is born of a woman is of few days, and full of trouble."

"He cometh forth like a flower and is cut down, he fleeth also as a shadow, and continueth not."

"Thou turnest man to destruction, and sayest, Return, ye children of men."

"Thou carriest them away as with a flood; they are as a sleep; in the morning they are like the grass which groweth up."

"In the morning it flourisheth and groweth up, in the evening it is cut down and withereth."

"We spend our years as a tale that is told."

"My days are swifter than a weaver's shuttle."

"The days of our years are three score years and ten, and if by reason of strength they be fourscore years, yet is their strength labor and sorrow; for it is soon cut off, and we fly away."*

What choice texts to read, and improved so well, who does not remember, on funeral occasions! The New Testament is not free from a like infirmity. We hear mention of the body as "vile," and the feeling is of disesteem for this life, as a dreary pilgrimage, a dark fate, and the hope is centered on the world beyond, where is recompense and deliverance. It is plain that where such disparagements prevail there has not been the true reading either of time or eternity. It would seem as if in some of the old ages there had been a general obliquity

* Job 14: 1, 2. Psalm 90: 3, 5, 6, 9. Job 7: 6. Psalm 90: 10.

of vision, an *amaurosis* indeed, so that the world of existence could not be seen or known in just sense at all. The more practical and healthful Western mind has been affected with it almost alike deeply with the Eastern. It has covered earth like a pall, and the obscuration, as we see, is not removed yet.

Buddha may have been, quite likely was charged with this taint. It certainly marred the completeness of his character. He was of the dark temperament, as the tradition gives him, pensive and sombre by nature, so penetrated and overcome with feeling of the infinite, that he was lost to sense of the world of the seen. "All is perishable, all is miserable, all is void,"—is an expression that, judging by the tradition, must frequently have passed his lips. And yet, before we strongly condemn another, let us see to it that *we* be subject in no degree to a like reproach.

But, again, with all the phenomenal, the empty and unreal—and at hours how shadowy it all seems —*there is substance.* The world an apparition, a very Sheol above ground, it is also *real.* We look into the faces in the street as they flit by, how apparitional they seem; in the mellowed light of the past or the near future, what are they? Shadow of a shade, ghosts, dreams and dreamers all. Flesh is dust, life is a vapor. And yet do we feel there is something far more. The gaze penetrates, fixes us. Here are vital relations. This mortal is putting on immortality, it is immortal. The phenomenal is substantial and everlasting. The great qualities certainly abide, and love, magnanimity, devotion are beyond peradventure, no spectral illusion. These faces are radiant, these masks reveal, and these transient shows beam deep with meaning as of the being of God. And so the friendships and the friends are abiding, become more real than ever, as reading through the sensuous and illusive, seeing all in symbol, we penetrate to substance, the inner truth of all. How grandly sacred becomes to us a person! We are awe-stricken, intensely solemnized. Before us a clothed eternity, a Theophania, clothed and also veiled; fleeting, momentary, and also everlasting; patent to sense, and also utterly inaccessible, beyond the power of hand to touch, or any organ to know. How fine and tender these relations; we are pervaded with restraint and reverence; hushed be every passion or sensuous feeling. Who could think of violating in smallest point this temple of the soul? Before that shrine we bow, as before the majestic Presence of Divinity.

Buddhism, doubtless, was guilty of short-coming here, as what great faith of the world has not been? All have stumbled at that stumbling-stone. None have yet read well, none attained the fine interpretation. Pythagoras, of all the prophets we know, has gone farthest in essay towards accomplishment in this most difficult work. Zoroaster also seems to have approximated beyond any other name in the East. Buddhism went to the highest heights of negation, bore its protest powerfully and well, but did not reach the affirmation. Let it be judged in this regard fairly, nothing extenuated, and no measure of condemnation meted out to it that is not given to other faiths chargeable with like deficiency.

It is not easy to say of its renunciation, speaking of it entire, how far it was healthy or had healthy elements, and how far of morbid tinge, whether the withdrawal was for concentration and conquest, true work, or for escape. There is much that we need to cast aside that we may be light-weighted to run the race before us. Every impediment, every clog we must away with, everything that delays us from climbing swiftly the road upward to God. There are stern lessons to be put here, and no preacher has yet laid emphasis on them too strongly. But there is sometimes also pusillanimity, desire to abdicate our relations, to withdraw from the post of life. Existence here is a conflict, and it requires some effort even to live. There come hours perhaps to all, when the soul prays, "May this cup pass from me," when the resolution fails, the mountain looms too high, and it asks to be relieved; it would to naught and death. Perhaps the Buddhistic doctrine took on something of this type, we cannot quite say at this distance. But we can see it a grave mistake, involving a totally wrong apprehension of life from the bottom, not better and not worse, as appears, than the current conception of salvation and heaven as implying deliverance and exemption from all responsibilities and labors that come so ungrateful here. The deliverance is not by withdrawal, but by conquest. Rest itself is motion; repose, the perfection of action.

Life itself is such a battle, there is no escape but by victorious doing. Every morning summons us to a new conflict, every day brings new surprises, requirements, tasks not anticipated. The nails will grow, the pores will transpire, the body, as also the mind, undergoing constantly transmutation. There is no cessation to the work of disintegrating; necessity there is for perpetual conflict, resistance and struggle to hold against the flood and keep good by renewals the waste. Each individual in life is like one upon ocean in a frail and leaky bark, to be kept afloat only by incessant exertion. He must pump or die. All that we have acquired or possess goes continually to detorioration, enemies on all hands attack it, lay waste, and there must be unwearying effort to repair and maintain. Eternal vigilance is here the price of every liberty. Whoso would abdicate this incessant struggle must go out of his own body, out of existence itself. There is no exemption to aught that dwells in time.

"Life's no resting but a moving,"—

This Buddhism ought, if it did not, to have seen and made good recognition of.

For here we touch upon great issues, the vital questions of life open at this door. The deliverance is by exaltation and enlargement, mastery until motion is perfect rest, and our activity becomes free, victorious, spontaneous as the breath. There is to be no effort and no weariness. The Nirvâna is possession; the felicity, life more and more expanded and exalted. That we feel embarrassed and find ourselves burdened and shackled, is proof of our weakness. We have not yet become seized of our estate. When we shall have been, we shall have no longing or unrest, nothing can be hard or painful, we shall feel never for a moment disposition to retire or escape any work or requirement. Conflict shall transmute into conquest; in all the circumstances about us, not one thing unfriendly. Without indifferference, we shall yet be without solicitude or any pain. The large soul loves and works largely, with zest and serene joy. Indisposition for labor, shrinking from its trials and responsibilities is, perhaps, always a mark of impaired vitality; it betokens imbecility or advancing old age. Very frequently indeed it is in close connection with diseased physical condition, and hardly knows cure short of the removal of that. Taking in view the high mark, how few of us, indeed, reach or even approach the period of twenty-one! Few approximate the fine golden mean, find the true reconciliation and marriage of seen and unseen, undertaking never too much, neither too little, never indifferent and never borne away, pursuing, and keeping and deepening perpetually in the pursuit, the inward rest.

There may fitly be discrimination and selection. All are not anointed to every work. With each individual there should be deliberate judgment and choice of his vocation. There is also gradation and a relativity of values, and there may be, there must be preferences. One claim stands subordinate to another. Remembering the gradation and constant ascension, we should keep lower subservient and cheap beside the higher. There may be setting aside in a measure of the grosser tasks, in order to a larger dedication and freer performance of higher work. One should not spend his life in doing, however devotedly, on trifles or matters of inferior moment. Every day we are called to weigh, to take the comparative measurements, and adjust ourselves to fresh claims. That which was paramount and commanding yesterday may be subordinate to-day. Every hour frequently shifts values, and it requires great skill, as well as fine judgment, to make the instant adjustments. We may well feel ill at ease with ourselves, if we use not good discrimination and selection. There must be a singleness and soleness in all effective dedication, a shutting out of all rivals from the homage, the devotion of the worshiper. Much may be excused to the superior genius who separates himself largely from the manual labors, that he may do finer and more. And yet none may withdraw himself utterly; every man must keep burnished and bright the link that unites him with the world of the material and his toiling fellows, must keep alive some taste of the labor involved to provide for the primal necessities. Withdrawal, in this sort, will vitiate the quality of his thought, impair the bond of sympathy through which he sees, knows and enters into the condition of men, and be very apt also to harm his character. The more exalted one's soul, the more royally and inspiringly he can do. All tasks may transmute into pastime and delight under his hand. His companionship, on any field, is an exhilaration. No man may rightfully forget, while in the body, that he has a body, and that he primarily should serve and feed his own. It is to be suspected that Buddhism made its grave, its fatal short-coming here. This blemish seems to mar all the great saintships thus far in history. The monk, with staff and alms-bowl asking for bread, is not quite honorable or manly in the midst of working mankind. He that is least in the kingdom of Heaven is greater than he. He that strives to sustain truly and well the relation to wife, family, society, that conquers on that plane, writes and realizes—he has fought a higher battle, and stands in this point greater than all renunciants. And in the household he may learn lessons, behold revelations finer and deeper than Buddha saw in his solitude.

The requirement for all is that none in any labor shall become absorbed and lost. And none must abdicate or think for a moment of retiring from exertion. Any work, however coarse or ungrateful to the feeling, is infinitely better than none. All has in it divine elements, and may be transmuted to beauty and song. *Do something*, and keep mind and heart ever alive. "I feed," says Giordano Bruno, "upon the high endeavor." There is no rust so fatal as the rust of inaction. The old hymn hath it

—— 'only while we pray, we live.'

In larger and stricter sense, only while we *act*, we live. Even old age may be animated by a purpose, and the years of infirmity may—should be—occupied with interests and work. An aim is antiseptic, it resists the invasion of decay. There is no such anodyne for the ills and pains of life as absorption of the attention on worthy objects. Each one should seek, in however advanced years, when the hour comes, to die in the harness. "Give me a great thought, that I may be quickened with it while I die," said the expiring Herder to his attendant.

And even the secondary or inferior may become, for the time being at least, paramount, and the man of highest spiritual gift, with great calling to teach, to prophesy, may see occasion that shall imperatively summon him to the toilful hand-laborer's life, a vocation to be preferred immeasurably before any mean surrender or degradation. He will find that here, too, the divine enrichments will come, that sootiest toil will permit, aye, bring inspirations, great communion, open to broadest culture and enlargement, that no favored position bought at price of manly erectness can begin to give. There are advantages purchased at fatal price, and they shrink to dry ashes in the hand.

VI.

THE FINE PROBLEM.

THE right apprehension of this world, seeing all things as they are, in their duality and their oneness, correlating time with the eternal, keeping the fact and the true subordination — this is ever the question of questions, the one problem of human life. Buddhism brings us to it, all historic studies, especially of faiths and institutions, bring us to it. This once solved, the human being has done his errand, wrought out his destiny and entered into final rest.

It is a very old question, considered and experimented upon through all the ages. How use the world, never abusing it, how make the just recognitions, avoiding renunciation and escape absorption, how love and embrace as we must, but never setting too much stake in the object — this is the severe problem. If I would be just, making full recognition of all the claims of the outer and seen, relations to the world of time, I fall into forgetfulness and idolatry; if I would guard well and keep clear, I become tainted with indifference, a renunciant, a withdrawn and ghastly saint. On the Scylla or the Charybdis all barks go to wreck, or from the one to the other, many all the life long vainly toss and beat.

The outer is not matter of indifference, and the material condition, the physical or mundane basis, is not to be despised or disregarded. Outer and inner, corporeal and ethereal are clamped together in this world by indissoluble bonds. Lower leads to and culminates in higher, and there is no higher that does not stand and rest in lower. The matter of circumstances in reference to the house, the appointments of the home, may seem trivial, at least unimportant, and yet the neglect of one little particular may cost a life, may bear to the shades irrecoverably the face of a dear one. We must distinguish while we cannot separate, discriminate and hold fitly in place, while we cannot put asunder. It is so very delicate a task, speculatively impossible, practically most difficult, seeming unattainable.

Every thing must be put upon the scales and marked at its just value, or the approximation, and the valuation needs to be revised and re-marked continually as the relations change, which they do every day and every hour. There must be constant use of the balance, and ever-returning reference to the absolute standard. How the values change according to the perspectives we look through, that which seems so large and commanding in view of the near present, shrinking into insignificance and naught in view of the long future. And there is variation in the standard within at different moments, days and periods of life; at least it comes out some times with greater distinctness, is more pronounced, clear, vital, than at others. And the highest norm is at best but an approximation, only a comparatively just scale; there is some *amaurosis* always, points of insensibility in the nerve, *mirage* in the eye, chromatic refractions. At the highest heights the vision is partial, the angels are chargeable with folly. But if we advance, there are constantly new corrections, finer sensibilities being wakened within ourselves.

The puzzle seems to be to avoid excess, to keep to the limit. The way is slippery, and the descent to Avernus so easy. There is such constant expansion to the wants, or what we conceive to be our wants, such quick, rising intensity. One sets out to build the house; the requirements so grow and multiply, there are so many things that suggest, it were well, aye, necessary, to have them—the dimensions swell ere we are aware, out of all proportion to the land we must build on, or the purse we must build from. And the appointments, the furnishing of the house with its various wares, necessary, convenient, elegant—how they enlarge and increase till literally there is no end. The absorptions are so great, so subtle, that ere one is aware, he is borne from his feet and lost in the vortex. No house ever gets finished, no estate is ever large enough, and no appointments quite complete. The accumulation of materials in the course of years—how it swells up! Be careful as one will, the collection will grow and extend, implements, materials for use, articles of the household, shop, or farm economy, laid aside, not of any present need, yet not willingly thrown away. A fire, a removal, a relentless auction, may clear away the superfluous stuffs, but in absence of one or another of these, what steadily increasing bondage is brought! We become encased in a hard shell, layer after layer, incrustations that bind us tight and forbid all fluidity and freedom. How many a housekeeper becomes, ere she is aware, held and kept by her house, how many an estate owner, owned by his estates! And so the multitudes of men and women in our society, our active and advanced civilization, are brought under deep idolatries and shackles of an inextricable bondage. Is there no method of having any thing without being possessed, chained and hampered by it? Is there no medium between subjugation and renunciation; no freedom but in being a *sans culotte?*

Habitude, the accustomed ways and surroundings, have power for ill as well as good, perhaps more than for good. Use and wont confine and enslave us. We grow to the habitual, the scenes and experiences of the every-day life, till we become identified with them, they are a part of ourselves. We cannot break from them, are fastened, incarcerated, unable to move at the call of the spirit. The languid nature cries, "Let me first go and bury my father." I see, not without dread, the power of this element, especially as the years advance, and the enthusiasm, elasticity and warm courageous spirit of youth have diminished. We incline to the accustomed, to rest in what we have, unwilling to break away and forth to new fields and larger work. Every day adds a cord to the fastening, and erewhile the toil becomes so strong we cannot possibly break it. Every man as he enters age, tends to become contracted, conservative, a fogy. The blood retires more inward to the heart, he is less disposed to exertion, to aggressive forward movement. His cry is, "Let alone, let be, no disturbance, no disruption." He is glued to his objects; when they are taken, like Laban he has lost his gods. Only as he keeps his blood warm and quick, his pulse beating with the life of the world, can he escape.

Our relations to the *social* involve us in grave

exposure. How these faces write, this presence of the dear ones of the household, the friendly circle—what a power it has to touch and affect us to the quick! The impressions are so vital, they enter the very life-centers. All unconsciously we are borne away with a wild idolatry. We identify the form with the substance, the expression with the reality, we forget the symbolism. A single experience may be fraught with danger, the glance of the eye, the beam in the look, the word which is music to the ear—how it may carry us captive and bear away. I note with awe sometimes and shrinking fear these fascinations, the allurements, the fine, transporting charms of the home circle, and apprehend lest they become too dear, too essentially indispensable in their habitual manifestation, to the soul's enjoyment. All unconsciously our hearts' loves are entwined there so deep, we live in and of them, and cannot bear separation. But the separation comes, as it must, ever has and ever will, and we are bereft indeed. Our lode-stars are gone, the light of our life blotted out. Death strips us of our delights, and we sit in darkness, saddened, alone.

And yet there is a medium line to be hit; we are individuals and are each an incarnated spirit, breathing and dwelling in time, and some garments we must have, we cannot go naked in this world.

We have relations and dependencies, we must converse and commune. How mingle and still hold superiority, how recognize and honor, warm to and love, and get upon us never a trace of a shackle? We want the wise teacher who shall elucidate, show us the reconciliation and true deliverance. Repose in action, repose that acts and activity that reposes—is the need of every day and every hour of every life.

In the old Vedic Hymns, early almost apparently as the dawn of any civilization among men, any social, tamed, human life, going back to the days when agriculture was hardly born, settled life in houses just beginning or young, man poor almost as a naked savage, existence a perpetual struggle, such as we can hardly conceive of now, we find invocations to the superior powers and forces of nature, for supply of the most elemental wants. Give us possessions, food, shelter, family, and continued life here, O Indra! We crave remembrance in the body, in the imperative resistless needs of our physical being. The staple of these old hymns, deeply religious as they are, is still grossly material, showing man glued to the earth, groveling amid its absorptions, in the first stages only of his birth into consciousness of the higher. His eyes begin to open upon the great realities, he is filled with wonder, with aspiration, superlative longing, but the hard necessities encase him, and he falls back ever and anon to the stern needs that press him without, the measureless distance that divides him from the desired and the indispensable material possession. Man an infant, a naked child, exposed, beset, hampered, and in life-and-death struggle with enemies, unable to overcome his pressures, ravished, but too weak to rise to the upper airs and dwell in exaltation and repose—this is the spectacle presented to us in that early, almost primitive stage of human history.

We stand now at distance of forty, or perhaps more centuries from that,* the struggles, advances and enlargements of so many ages behind us, man the heir of all the attainment of this past, risen from naked savagery to a clothed and comparatively fine civilization—and yet have we grown much from that old condition? All abroad the same cry goes up continually: Give us possessions, O Heaven! We want means, wealth, property and power, an emancipated, protected and favored life. What emphasis upon the food to eat, the clothes to wear, in one view essential condition, but as held largely, merest incident,

* Bunsen says the oldest of the Vedas, the purely popular, cannot be younger than 3000 B. C. See Max Müller's *Chips*, Vol. III., p. 471; also Bunsen's *Egypt*, Vol. V., p. 562.

and even fatal snare. Such constant occupation with the material relations, perpetual study and labor for change and advantage and power here. In any true rendering in invocation of the absorbing desires and effort of to-day, hardly less prominent place would be covered by the prayers for possession and physical supply, than we find in those old rude petitions of the early Aryan ancestors. With all the wealth, the enhanced comfort and emancipation, the goal is still unneared, and we may say even unsighted. Man still grovels on the earth, unable to rise and take the freedom, the great repose that is his birthright. It is yet the dispensation of the first man, of the earth, earthy.

The same character is stamped upon our public civilization. So patent, it is obvious to all eyes. The material element seems excessive, so dominant as to make deformity and distortion. Such eagerness, haste of work, rush and impatience after performance and outer conquest. Visit any of the marts of trade, routes of commerce, shops of business, and you see everywhere the fevered life, gigantic movements that would stir from their places the very heavens, immense enterprises carried forward to aggrandize and fill with power. The brute forces of nature are commanded into service, and steam, electricity, heat, winds, are made to do the bidding of man in this quest. Probably there is not a force in the bowels of the earth, in the atmosphere, or the stars, that will not be captured and tamed to this use. Human life is rapid, breathless with ambition and speed in all the incidents of outer wealth and achievement. Look at the thoroughfares, and you see the eager rush of everybody to go abroad, to traverse the planet, myriads whirling on with the speed of the wind, and in perpetual stream — no rest and no goal. You are impelled to interrogate, Wherefore? Whence do all these come, and whither are they bound? Was there ever the like thirst and universal movement before? The brain of man is in constant gestation, travailing perpetually with inventions and skilled devices for subduing time, annihilating the space separations, and conquering to his feet the world.

The same dream of possession seems to haunt the scientific domain, the same thirst and unrest, and the glasses are armed with ever-increasing power, that they may see to the end of finitude, probe and explore all the height and depth of the unmeasured universe. Never was there such hope and assured expectation, such tension and energizing of every faculty. Not unnaturally, perhaps, is the head dazed with the great successes, wonderful of late, beyond any parallel hitherto, and the intoxication comes in that dreams, that this daring, conquering intellect of man is on the eve of piercing and laying open the final secret of secrets.

Viewing from one point of observation, we may say that there is fate, destiny here. It must needs be so. There are conditions yet to be fulfilled, certain preliminary terms to a true spiritual mastery, that must be answered, and the race is moving on, in large part unconsciously, to work an indispensable mission, to smooth and make straight the way for the coming of the Most High. Man is not yet free enough on the physical plane, he is the creature of stern necessities that bind him, too preöccupied, absorbed, harried, too much still in the exposure and lack of primitive savagery, to be able to command himself to withdrawal and inner repose. See what exposure in the person, what bankruptcy of health and life, what premature decay, what sorrows, what heavy odds against which perpetually to contend! What a tragedy is life all about us, what an unceasing, relentless battle, what clouds, what sadness visit! There is still sternest destitution and need, the requirement to fight and to wrest whatever we would win; much also that, with all the bravery of fight, we are unable to get. The great battle with weakness, want, with cold, disease and sharp pressures is still to be done, ere, as would seem, the higher life is to any large extent possible. Destiny has charged its ministers with this performance, and the word shall surely accomplish that whereunto it was sent.

Sad enough it is to see of some, that they appear so delicately constituted, there is such lack of just poise in their temperament, such over-proportion even of the finer, the spiritual, that they are unfitted to bear the rude shocks of the experiences of time, and so go down broken and crushed, summoned out of life ere they have been able to read and get its lessons. The flower was too delicate for the winds that blew, and the storms that sometimes come, and could not therefore fill the measure of its days and reach its full perfection. Nature was too harsh for this sensitive plant; the earth itself seems still rude and in a sort sinister to human life. A withering breath comes and destroys. Of others, too, we must feel that they are so charged with down-weighing infirmities, some bias, some torpor or perversion, that amid all tuitions of experience, they never will attain, never reach good birth, but, as a vulgar phrase hath it expressively, they "die a-bornin." Both these short-comings or miscarriages are very tragic, and long ages of thought and careful toil must be passed, ere they shall occur no more.

It is to be hoped, indeed, that some day, not distant, will witness material reduction in the stern, exacting manual labors that lie to all honest hands. The pressure and necessary absorptions are great. Large portion of our waking hours in a climate, so rigorous as ours, where, emphatically, for most part,

"The winter consumes what the summer doth yield,"

must be given, as we now are, to the meat that perisheth, to food, shelter, providence. We have begun a little on some planes to organize, to associate and make distribution of the labors, but largely we are unorganized, unequipped, and are laboriously doing at the hardest, with muscle and nerve, what some day shall be taken up and performed more than willingly by forces that lie wild and sporting untamed about us. We are still in the old stone age, the finer metallic ages yet unborn. The whole creation groaneth and travaileth in pain until now, waiting to be delivered. The men of science to-day are performing, in part probably unknown to themselves, an important, an indispensable mission in the attention they are calling to, and the light they are to bring upon, a side of human life all too much ignored and neglected hitherto.

But again, taking our stand on the plane of the moral, we can see that great lessons are to be read and appropriated even now. Are we under no intoxication, do we never exaggerate, put things out of proportion, worship never the *eidolon*? Are there no unrest, no anxieties, extravagant, illusive hope and inordinate pursuits? Do we always keep to the fine maxim, "*Festina lente*," find constantly repose in our action here? It would seem that the intoxication of the quest has become so great that we have forgotten ourselves, lost the meaning of our object, and are unable to recall our grey-hounds and pause, even when the chase is done and the game is brought. We have gotten to the goal we started to win, but our dizzy eyes see not that it is any goal. Life is full of these oblivions, ends forgotten and ignored even when they have come into our hands. There need stern admonitions here, even though they should come by the severe surgery of excision, utter renunciation. All are too much imprisoned, excited and absorbed. We are cumbered with much serving. There must be peace, ceasing from care and solicitudes, the harrying of unrest. The kingdom of deliverance we must enter *now*.

The design seems in our present condition to be largely discipline, and through that, strength. The creature was born subject to vanity, to limitations and illusions, that he might attain, gain rest by effort, acquisition, and also by renunciation. Freedom we are to find in the midst of our shackles, breaking many, and of others discovering how insignificant they are, how little, indeed naught, they needs must hamper us. There appears but one door to the upper realm, and that is exertion and conquest. It seems the fiat of fate, covering all the future possibilities, that man can enjoy only as he shall have earned; he must do, to be able to enter into rest.

In high sense, too, the enjoying *is* the earning, and the resting the working. In the present stage and under the present relations, there may be enfranchisement, peace; who shall say they may not be perfect? Certainly there is great enlargement and repose in learning what we may do without, where we may enter upon inner substance, and find meanings and nourishment we had never suspected before. Man thus becomes a sovereign; though he seems a bondsman, a manacled slave, he is possessor and lord of all. The two spheres of life so interlap, or rather meet, unite, and run together without seam or suture, their mingling is so perfect, that it is not easy often to determine where the passive virtues properly end, and the active begin, or *vice versa*. The attainment of this were the perfect knowledge, making the supreme haven. The one side or the other comes more prominently to view in the various relations, and yet both are involved in every relation, and in the performance of every act. Devotion and surrender, pursuit on the one side, yielding up on the other, is the necessity of every hour. To have the flow perfect, the liberty and the allegiance absolute, no division and no unrest in the soul, but unbroken peace—this is the art of arts.

In the large, the problem before us is a very broad and far-reaching one, for it involves the consideration of the mysteries, the reconciliation of eternity and time. What we have touched upon is but one phase, and the more obvious and almost superficial, of our great question. How shall we reconcile, how eliminate the inferior factor, or rather sublimate and absorb it, pouring it for exaltation and strength even, into the higher? How blend the two spheres, and put the outer and the seen perfectly into the unseen? Toiling ages work upon it, yet it goes unanswered, unsolved forever.

"A rampart breach is every day
Which many mortals are storming,
Fall in the gap who may,
Of the slain no heap is forming."

The question remains, the subtle riddle of philosophy, the hidden, inaccessible mystery of being. Patent and radiant to all, quenching every other sight and fact, and yet so transcendent it will not be found or touched. No sage or seer has yet offered us any elucidation. We catechise all masters, none has framed answer; little hints touching some rim or remote edge of our question, pregnant intimations of the direction in which alone the true discovery may be found — these are all that the wealth of any history can give us. The true elucidator, solver, would be a sage far wiser than Plato, a saint higher, diviner than Jesus. But it is idle to speculate, ungracious to *seem* even to complain that we have not received the impossible. Such prerogative cannot be delegated for any soul to another. All that can be given is feeble hint, dim, distant intimation of this unseen, this one

> 'Unspeakable, who sits above these heavens,
> To us invisible, or dimly seen,
> In these his lower works.'

One or another in the long ages has read a note in this celestial music, has deciphered a syllable or two in this scripture of untold wisdom. But the reader that shall penetrate and translate it all, rendering into our vernacular, the performer that shall bring to our ears the divine harmonies, the eternal anthem of the heavens — the generations wait him evermore in vain. Not Jews only, but mankind, look for such Messias that should come. "My religion," said Lao Tsze, so wisely, "consists in thinking the inconceivable thought, in going the impassable way in speaking the ineffable word, in doing the impossible thing."

The attainment lying in character, the approximations must be very partial, remote with the best. The wisest among us outgrow the illusions but very gradually. The intoxications have affected all heads, the dark Lethe waters have been drunk by all, and we are smitten with forgetfulness, not so much of the life in time, but of the life in eternity. We outgrow, one after another, our day dreams and exaggerations, and get our feet upon the more solid ground, see things in their proportion. But hardly at all do we find any ultimate; world opens within world continually, and there is ever the transcendent and beyond. Oldest and wisest are but children of a larger growth, and as to-day we look back upon the illusions of the early years, wondering the intoxications could have been so easy and complete, so, erewhile, we shall doubtless recur with the same surprise to the dreams and enchantments of our seemingly now adult life. Are we not all in the stages of childhood, all undergoing, frequently enough with much pain, the processes of birth, and the eyes widest seeing not yet ripened to good vision?

What humility and what patience with all others we ought to learn in this view! Pythagoras said, "Esteem it a great part of a good education, to be able to bear with the want of it in others." Probably at the end, or rather in the beyond, we shall find that we have continued throughout idolaters, inebriated, exaggerating our own life even, worshiping unduly what has seemed essential condition to all existence and possession. It also shall be seen unessential, but an incident, not vitally touching the inner elements of our being.

And within that great illusion, how many minor illusions find place, and bear us captive continually. So instinctively the heart fastens here and there, and regards a thing as vital and follows it, or, balked and thwarted, grieves over the disappointment, forgetting the Nirvâna, forgetting that the resources of the universe are infinite, and that to the real soul there can come no loss, no sorrow. Our occupations, our life designs, how inseparable from the absolute ends they seem to us, how we cling to and invest in them, how we are pained or disheartened by their interruption or disappointment! Passes there a day with any of us in which the sun does not undergo some partial obscuration, in which we are not dazed or drugged and lost in forgetfulness? The reality is a Proteus, taking infinity of shapes and no shape, ever eluding and beckoning on.

Circumstance is made indifferent, the infinite possibilities all. Art thou called being a slave, said Paul, care not for it. We must not be thwarted, not *affected* even, by our incidents, must hold to the purpose, must execute the purpose, visibly, or at least inwardly, in spite of every untoward surrounding. It is high attainment so to dwell in perfect poise, that there shall come no ruffling or unrest, befall what may. You pursue your thought; the aim is noble, commanding. It is pleasant that the visitors come, that the inspirations flow and the mind be filled, illumined, propelled as by sovereign, all-mastering power. But the visitors may not come, the mind sit barren, uninspired, and the hour sacredly dedicated, yield nothing. To dwell in repose there also, to rest where you cannot act, acquiesce where you cannot obtain, feel content and assured even there, satisfied that this also is well, is best — it needs strength, self-command for that.

It helps us on in our way, to extend the period, to fix our thought on the perennial. We need to lengthen out the perspective. We see that things are not what they seem, that a larger range reduces them more into just proportions. Past will bloom still present, present fades, and beams in its inner realities alone upon us as past, future comes present, and we dwell in the eternal now. Hardly can we be pierced by any sorrow, for in the world we inhabit death and bereavement cannot enter. We cannot be affected by any ebriety, for the waters have been purged of all their intoxicating qualities.

The doctrine of fate also has its uses. It is well to remember that what is best, will be. There is election, a decree from the foundation of the world, and come what will, try what may, I shall doubtless have and find what I was destined for. Nothing can pluck out of that hand. Unsatisfactory occupation, absorbing, uncongenial business engrossment, place seeming not the right one for the capacity, not congruous or friendly, surroundings and position all awry—these cannot thwart or prevent that the actual destiny be realized. All can be transmuted, and made not hindrances, but doorways and aids to help us on to God. And it is probable that at the end, all our life will be seen to have been presided over by a beneficent fate. All will have been spent amid disappointments and also surprises, we seeming to ourselves. to be habitually balked of our wishes, consigned and compelled to work and experiences not chosen, not grateful, praying sometimes that this cup may pass from us, to awaken at length to see that he whom we sought was in this place, but we knew it not, that the great possession was always accessible, at hand, and that whatever we have failed to realize was by our own fault, aye, that we have been led by a way that we knew not, and have realized, have plucked wisdom and felicity more than we thought or imagined at the time. So the kingdom of the skies is patent to all, and every relation, however humble or hard with trial, permits, nay, favors, nay, effects, the growth of the heavenly fruits and joys.

Doubtless, a considerable part of our embarrassment has its ground in our constitution, the very conditions of our being. We are in limits, are ourselves limited. The desires, the dissatisfactions we feel, come essentially not of this or that particular type of circumstance, any special trammel or hamper of condition, but of our nature. These thirsts within us are to be slaked in the infinite ocean alone. While we are short of that, there will always be some sense of lack or pain. We are not greatly to blame any special condition we are in, for what belongs essentially to finitude. Withal we must surrender and renounce at some points, or we cannot realize anywhere. Life requires a concentration; it is a spark, a focal point, a determinate aim. This is one of the essential laws or terms of a personal existence. The high art is to adjust one's self finely to the possibilities, to yield what cannot be kept and carried, and have the perfect peace still unbroken. When we have taken survey and entered upon devotion to all our possible, when we have surrendered without pain, with alacrity and solemn joy, whatever is impracticable or not commanding or worthy, and withal wed ourselves to interest and action—then we take our inheritance and enter into life.

There shall be no abdication of the normal relations. The thing sought shall be appropriation, absorbing and exalting all the lower into the higher. We do not want negation. Nothing normal must be dropped or lost. The gospel of renunciation has been preached powerfully enough in our own time by Thoreau. None could urge its claims with more eloquence and force than he. Earlier ages have witnessed like confessors adjuring to forsake and renounce, bearing their testimony against dwelling and mingling in a world unworthy. It has been a weighty, an indispensable word. It has admonished of things much neglected and to which all should take heed. It has reminded us of our excesses and our bondage. But the world to-day needs more and larger, the inclusive affirmation. It looks for the synthesis, the great reconciliation. This is the at-one-ment for which the ages have been preparing. Æons of time, untold centuries of endeavor, of sacrifice and suffering, are cheap that might ripen a period for its advent, its realization.

Partial as it is, the past is pregnant with hint and needed incitement. There are fingers all along in history that point the way. There have been incarnations, souls in flesh that have brought the heavens to the earth, and constrained men to say, "Immanuel, God with us." How gladly would we listen to the faintest word from Buddha, from Jesus, showing that he too had weighed the vast problem, and held some careful conclusions thereon, that he had wrought upon it, and reached a never so remote approximation! Very deep is the debt we owe to the Oriental, particularly the Indian thinkers and dreamers, those men who in the old days so essayed to solve the deep riddle, sought to withdraw and emancipate themselves, retiring from the world, from the body, from the very life even, that they might gaze purely upon being. The old sages pierced through form and spectacle, saw the sea of illusion, *Mâyâ* and all things floating thereon, a very *mirage* in the desert. They sought to penetrate to substance, to reach the within of all the within, to rest in formless and unchanging. They sought to transcend, to read all in the permanent relation, nothing in the transient, to dwell in the everlasting now. There is no second example like it; never has the human mind so divested itself and soared in the ether, in the heavenly spaces, and out of space and beyond time, as in India. This also was needed as a protest, a check and counterpoise to the intense sensuousness, the devotion to outer objects and enjoyments, of the multitudes of mankind. It was needed to proclaim the presence and power of the ethereal, the heavenly, amid all the noise, glare and bewitchment of the earthly. The Greek thought was brother, born of the same womb, later in its appearance, more realistic, cognizant of form and the time determinations, but in the great brains like Pythagoras, Parmenides, Plato, hardly less sublime in its aerial flights.

Born in that royal line was Gautama. He came with this heritage, his nerves thrilled to the infinite. True it was of him, as the biographer says of Giordano Bruno, "penetrated with consciousness of eternity." His soul soared into the everlasting, his heart beat to beauty and to love, his thought flowed into poetry, into anthems of song. He was so intoxicated with changeless and eternal, he forgot time and all of life here save the ethical law. Say if you will he was a short-coming, it was a lack-lustre landscape, a dreary blank, it was celebration of renunciation; criticise the limitations, the marked defects—we will confess it all; but he was a glorious accomplishment. His affirmation was love, self-surrender and self-sacrifice utter and absolute; he emphasized it so he lost all thought of person or of any determinate condition.

If he failed to realize and complete the work,

he stands by no means alone in that. Other prophets have fought to win the prize, have struggled to achieve, to rend the vail of the mystery, to elucidate and solve to complete and final demonstration. If he failed, we may remember the nature of the task, and consider that mortal can by no possibility here prevail. The inscription upon the Isiac image at Sais holds true evermore: "I am all that has been, is, and shall be, and no mortal hitherto hath lifted my vail."

Placed side by side with other great masters, he compares not unfavorably; none wrestled more strongly with the problems of being, none did and sacrificed greater for man, none aspired more yearningly to the goal of the infinite peace. Permanently the history must be regarded as another of the contributions towards solution of that, which in its own nature is supremely transcendent. That this prince of Kapilavastu, this monk of the Sâkyas, so wrought and endeavored bravely both in action and suffering, must also permanently entitle him to the thoughtful consideration and warm thanks of mankind. His resolute courage, his inflexible self-denial, and self-surrender, trampling upon every appetite and inclination, holding all things so sacred for the soul, shall pique, arouse, incite and draw all hearts near this high person in worship and in love. He became Siddhârtha

—"whose objects have been accomplished"—became Buddha—'whose eyes are wide opened,'—and multitudes of souls warmed by this presence, shall strive to calm the desires and attain the anointed vision. Beneath the tree at Bôdhimanda he saw; long journey any of us might well afford to make, to find that tree beneath which we should become full awake. In the spiritual experience, we find ourselves to this man near of kin. Continents, centuries of time, difference of blood and race cannot separate us.

But form and individual depart, all that is personal and historic passes away. This mortal is putting on immortality, is being sublimated perpetually into reality which is greater and more than it. "The name of Buddha is nothing but a word. The name of Bôdhisattva is nothing but a word."* Signal benefactors of the race, we know not in what numbers, already sleep in oblivion, no one can give us a vestige of their place or memory. Yet their work abides, the legacy goes on never to be consumed.

> "One accent of the Holy Ghost,
> The heedless world hath never lost."

---

*Burnouf, Introd., p. 481; quoted from the *Prajna Pâramitâ*, Absolute Wisdom.

Buddha may be, perhaps is already that, a myth, his history a tale of the imagination, but the career he wrought, the hint he dropped into the ear of the world, knows not death or decay. It has vitality with the life of God. All that is individual in the faith, the dispensation itself, shall wane and disappear, setting like stars from the sky, and superseded by a new day, but the idea, the Nirvâna, an eternal thought and aspiration, more than Buddha or his religion, shall ever illumine and quicken. Men shall work upon it, be filled by it, seek its infinite possession, long after all the names we know to-day, shall have faded from the memory of the world. Long as the race endures, as time exists, as the procession of the ages goes forward, so long shall the soul strive and aspire, pant to escape the bounds of limitation, climbing the giddy heights to reach the goal, to see and to be the changeless and the everlasting.

The growth in individual, in race, is slow, by very gradual and mostly imperceptible steps. The enlargement and exaltation come much through the experiences, one after another in life. These are the spirit flame and the water bath that set and bring into pronounced clearness the picture on the plate, the reminders that awaken remembrances of the forgotten home. The attainment is something organic. We see as we grow, mature age, make trial. We rise as we do, and through doing, for here eminently faith operates with works, and by works is faith made perfect. We catch glimpses which ripen more and more towards steady and clear vision. How intermit tingly the sun shines upon us, an instant of radiance, then periods of cloud and obscuration. But every slightest conquest tells, every step brings on, the sombre days also count, and the growth goes forward, much of it silent and unconscious, apparent only in the ulterior results.

We may be sure that the destiny of humanity is onward. The advance of each individual enters as an organic element, advancing and exalting the race. Better approximations shall be made, finer views, finer realizations, nearer and nearer approaches to the infinite goal. And in ages better than ours, generations shall be happier born, nobler bred, with more transparent flesh, purer blood and clearer brain, to whom our words shall seem childish, coarse, our conceptions dim and crude, who shall see where we but grope, shall walk and leap where we but hobble and totter and fall. The great atonement, reconciliation prepared from the foundation of the world, shall be wrought out, and life become absolute realization. In all the experience, not a sigh of sorrow, not a breath of unrest, never the rising of desire, no night there, perfect peace and perfect day.

But it shall be the same road ever, same method of approach, all things seen in relation, lower transcended and cast aside for higher, higher still found intact and entire amid all lowliest and poorest—attainment, surrender—pursuit, repose—time, eternity—till the goal which is beyond all goals is reached, conflict lost, aye, consummated in conquest, and the grave itself swallowed up in victory. The same reality and revelation ever—seen, unseen, blending, dividing, blending—ascending, flowing, soaring onward without end.

INDEX.

ERRATA.

On p. 49, second line from bottom, read "so as almost to cover it."
" 56, first line, put pause (comma) after "quickening."
" 70, second line from bottom, erase "the" before "every revenge."
" 122, the order of the foot notes should be reversed, and the reference mark against the second foot note (that now stands first) should correspond to the second reference mark in the text. A similar error in respect to reference marks occurs on next page (123).